INVESTING
FOR THE
FINANCIALLY
CHALLENGED

INVESTING
FOR THE
FINANCIALLY
CHALLENGED

WALTER UPDEGRAVE

WARNER BOOKS

A Time Warner Company

PUBLISHER'S NOTE: This publication is designed to provide competent and reliable information regarding the subject matter covered. However, it is sold with the understanding that the author and publisher are not engaged in rendering financial or other professional advice. Laws and practices often vary from state to state and if financial or other expert assistance is required, the services of a professional should be sought. The author and publisher specifically disclaim any liability that is incurred from the use or application of the contents of this book.

Warner Books, Inc., 1271 Avenue of the Americas, New York, NY 10020

Visit our Web site at www.warnerbooks.com

 A Time Warner Company

Printed in the United States of America

First Printing: June 1999

10 9 8 7 6 5 4 3 2 1

Library of Congress Cataloging-in-Publication Data

Updegrave, Walter L.
    Investing for the financially challenged / Walter Updegrave.
        p.   cm.
    Includes index.
    ISBN 0-446-67476-1
    1. Stock exchanges—United States.   2. Investments—United States.
    I. Title.
    HG4910.U63   1999
    332.6—dc21   98-50857
                                                                 CIP

Book design and text composition by L&G McRee
Cover design by Jon Valk
Cover illustration by Ron Barrett

To the two Muses I love most—Mary and Henry

CONTENTS

INVESTING
FOR THE
FINANCIALLY
CHALLENGED

Do You Suffer from Investaphobia?

• • • • • • • • • • •

E ver notice how perfectly intelligent, rational people go to pieces when it comes to investing?

It's true. We can excel in the most demanding of jobs, navigate the treacherous shoals of romantic relationships, even raise children without damaging their fragile psyches too badly. But when faced with something as simple as getting a decent return on the money we work so hard for, we don't have a clue.

Our eyes glaze over. Our attention wanders. The old mental processor just won't compute. To put it in technical terms, our brains turn to mush. But knowing we must do *something,* we do. We act on whim, make decisions based on mountains of misinformation, and eventually invest our hard-earned dough relying on the half-baked opinions of friends or family members, often people we wouldn't trust even to recommend a $1.99 video rental for a Saturday night.

Now what in the world could cause such utter hopeless confusion in sane, competent individuals like you and me? Well, I think the culprit is a widespread malady known as Investaphobia—a dread fear of all things financial that paralyzes our brains so completely, we make poor investing choices or none at all.

How do you know if you're a victim of Investaphobia? Do phrases like "prerefunded municipal bonds" and "collateralized mortgage obligations" immediately make your eyelids feel like they weigh a ton? If someone says, "Hey, I've got just the right large-capitalization value-oriented growth fund for you," do you hear, "I've got just the right la-la ka-ka-va-va-goo-goo foo-foo foam for you"? When you're at a cocktail party and the talk turns to mutual funds, do you find yourself nodding sagely as if you know what everyone's talking about when in fact you're searching desperately for the quickest escape route to the onion dip? If you answered yes to any of these questions—or if your brain gets fuzzy at the mere thought of dealing with your personal finances—then you (yes, you) may be in the grip of Investaphobia.

What causes this debilitating financial condition? No one knows for sure, but there are several less than fascinating theories. First of all, while money is fun to spend, let's face it, managing it can be pretty damn dull. So unless you're one of those geeky types who carries his Hewlett-Packard 12C financial calculator in a quick-draw hip holster, chances are you would submit to excruciating torture (like having sharp needles stuck beneath your fingernails or, worse yet, listening to a John Tesh concert) before you would spend twenty minutes analyzing stock mutual funds.

Another reason many of us are reluctant to spend any time thinking about the right way to invest is that, in their zeal to separate us from our money, the investment professionals who are supposed to make investing sensible for us often do the exact opposite—they make it vastly more confusing.

One way that Wall Street brokers, financial planners, and other investment advisers do this is by inundating us with a confounding blizzard of (largely unnecessary) investing products. At last glance there were more than 9,000 stock, bond, and money-market mutual funds vying for our attention (and probably another few hundred launched since you began reading this sentence), all seemingly claiming to be top performers by some self-serving standard or another (The All-Gain-No-Pain Fund Is Number One!*). Then there are the more than 3,400 stocks on the New York Stock Exchange, another 725 or so on the American Stock Exchange, and 3,900 more that are traded on the National Association of Securities Dealers' national over-the-counter market. You can follow these every day in the newspaper's stock tables, of course, if you don't mind getting a case of terminal eye strain as you try to decode what those microscopic numbers and letters next to their names mean.

An army of mostly commission-driven investment salesmen (and women) also bamboozle us by explaining these choices poorly and by talking about investments in an unintelligible patois that defies understanding. They throw out phrases like "coefficient of correlation" and "standard deviation" that seem to be made up of words in the English language but might as well be Esperanto, considering that few people (including some of the supposed experts who use them) know what they mean. To give you an idea of how lost many of us are when it comes to financial terms, consider this: A 1997 survey by the National Association of Securities Dealers found that while 78 percent of Americans could name a character on a TV sitcom, only 12 percent knew the difference between "load" and "no-load" mutual funds. Of course, the cynics among us feel that technobabble investment jargon is an integral part of Wall Street's game plan, an attempt to make the investment world seem so complex and confusing that we have no other choice but to rely on these pros as our investing saviors.

---

*If you look only at its return for the 3½ weeks ending September 3, 1998, and ignore the fact that it trailed similar funds over almost every other period of time.

Whatever the cause of Investaphobia, it's clear that millions of Americans suffer from it. You can often see the afflicted forking over commissions upward of 5.75 percent of what they invest to buy a mutual fund through brokers when they could easily have picked out just as good a fund, if not a better one, on their own and kept the commission in their own pocket. The worst cases, those in the advanced stages of Investaphobia, don't even know what they've invested in. Ask them, and you'll hear phrases like "It's a stock-annuity-variable-whatchamacallit plan." Or "It's a new company that's invented a, uh, nasal-spray cure for, uh, male pattern baldness . . . or was it bladder control? Whatever. All it needs is human testing."

THE ROAD TO FINANCIAL WELLNESS . . . AND WHY I'M JUST THE GUY TO PUT YOU ON IT

Enough of this depressing talk. Time to cheer up. Investaphobia isn't a terminal financial disease. In fact, it's not that hard to beat at all—provided you're willing to invest a little time and a little effort *before* you invest a lot of money. And this is just the book to put you on the road to financial wellness.

But first let's talk a bit about what qualifies *me* to do the job of transforming you from financially challenged to financially literate. After all, there are hundreds—no, thousands—of investment nabobs out there eager to tell you what to do with your money. Why listen to me?

Well, let me start with my most important qualification: *I'm not an investment professional.* That's right, I'm proud to say that I am not now—nor have I ever been—a broker, financial planner, money manager, or any other kind of investment counselor or Wall Street insider who collects a fee or commission for hyping a stock, selling a bond, or pushing a mutual fund. I've gained my knowledge of investing as someone who is an outsider in the investment world but who has spent a lot of time peering into it. No, I'm not a voyeur. But for more than fifteen years I've covered investing and personal finance as a journalist, most of those years for *Money* magazine. I've also invested my hard-earned dough, on my own, without help from investment professionals. So aside from my familiarity with the financial markets and my own investing experience, I'm really much like you: a reasonable, intelligent person who sees investing not as an end in itself, but as a means of achieving a better life.

The big advantage to my status as a sort of informed investment outsider is that I can give you a far more honest, sensible, and profitable investing strategy than what you would get from the Wall Street crowd. Most investing books, especially those written by investment pros, spend their time teaching you how to play the Wall Street game to win. They start with the premise that success lies in outsmarting the market and that you do that by emulating professional investors and traders. The truth is that most professional investors *don't* beat the market once you take into account all the fees and costs they generate with their fancy strategies. I contend that you win only when you *don't* play Wall Street's game. So I'll give you the information you need to set a strategy designed to benefit you, not an army of investment pros.

Another thing: Unlike many writers of investing books, I'm not trying to sell you specific investments or drum up clients for my brokerage or consulting or money management business. Ultimately, Wall Street boils down to one big sales machine. If it's not a broker or financial planner peddling stocks, bonds, or mutual funds, it's someone touting an investing strategy that requires lots of trading, which generates brokerage commissions. I'm not part of the Wall Street sales machine. The fact is, not many Wall Street pros will recommend this book; most will probably hate it. That's because to the extent that you follow my advice, brokers, money managers, and other pros will collect less money in the form of sales commissions, fees, and trading charges. Too bad for them.

So brace yourself for a radical departure from most investing books. Welcome to the first one with a bit of attitude. One that will help you cultivate a sense of skepticism that will enable you to realize when the conventional wisdom about investing is out-right bull—and when the Wall Street investment-and-sales machine is trying to snow you. Most important, this book will give you the information you need to invest sensibly on your own.

Other than that, I don't make any audacious claims for this book. But I will make four promises to you about the way I will write this book and about what it will help you do.

MY FOUR PROMISES

PROMISE #1: I'll be completely honest with you. If you're reading this book, you're obviously a person of intelligence and wit (after all, you're only *financially* challenged). So I'll treat you like a rational, intelligent adult. That means I won't bombard you with a lot of the pseudoadvice you find in other financial advice books and in many personal finance magazines that looks solid and authoritative but actually is impossible to follow. For example, I won't mislead you by claiming (or, more insidious, implying) that there's a way you can foresee a slump in stock prices, jump out of the stock market with big gains, "park" your cash in bonds or money-market funds, and then scoop up shares at bargain-basement prices just before another big rally. Rather, I'll show you how to build an investment portfolio that, while not immune to market setbacks, will limit your short-term losses to a level you can tolerate—and deliver solid long-term inflation-beating gains that will increase the purchasing power of your money.

PROMISE #2: I won't overload you with a lot of confusing, conflicting, and ultimately useless information you can't possibly factor into your investing decisions. Pick up some of the popular financial magazines or watch one of the financial shows on TV and you get the idea that to invest successfully you should be religiously poring over *The Wall Street Journal's* "Heard on the Street" column or tuning in every Friday to *Wall Street Week* to sift out nuggets of investment advice sandwiched between Louis Rukeyser's lame puns. Or that you need a Pentium processor brain capable of constantly absorbing price-earnings ratios, dividend yields, and every other stat you can stuff into your cerebrum.

Nonsense.

Truth is, most investment publications either paralyze you into indecision by dazing you with too much data or goad you into a frenzy of ineffective buying and selling by suggesting that you should be doing something *now!* with the supposedly sage advice they've just given you.

My theory: Sit back, relax, don't get caught up in the hurly-burly of the investment world. One of my working assumptions in this book is that, like me, you have a real life and you don't want to spend every spare second poring over supposedly sophisticated financial information that isn't likely to improve your investment gains anyway. So I'll give you sensible advice—essentially the same strategies I have used successfully in my own investing—that you can follow to get a good competitive return on your money without devoting your entire existence to monitoring your investment holdings.

PROMISE #3: I'll give you plenty of valuable investing guidelines and principles, but no magic formulas. Some investment experts suggest that the key to smart investing is watching the financial markets or the economy for signals that tell you when it's an opportune time to load up on or bail out of specific investments. You know the kind of nonsense I'm talking about: "If the spread between two- and thirty-year Treasuries exceeds three percentage points at the same time that the thirty-day moving average of pork belly futures hits an intramonth low, *Sell your house and put every dime you own into crude oil futures!*"

But I can tell you after more than ten years of researching such wonderful strategies as part of my job at *Money* magazine that there are two big problems with most of these systems: 1) you need the brain of a Nobel Prize–winning physicist to follow them; and 2) even if you could convince a Nobel laureate in physics to give you his brain, there's no assurance that the system will work in the future as well as it supposedly worked in the past.

Fact is, Wall Street is loaded with math wizards, or quants (for quantitative analysts), as they're called on the Street, who do nothing but play with their computers all day to find some combination of financial statistics that is supposed to lead to investing nirvana. (In Europe during the Middle Ages, these people were called alchemists.) But despite the high-octane brainpower that goes into all these investing systems, very, very few professional investors have proven themselves capable of beating the stock market averages for long periods of time—and predicting in advance who those rare skillful (or, in many cases, lucky) souls will be is even tougher. Instead of sophisticated-sounding formulas, I'll suggest easy-to-follow ways to increase your wealth that have worked for me and can work for you as well.

PROMISE #4: I won't titillate you with lists of mutual funds, stocks, or other investments that are supposed to "double your money!" in a few years. Stripped of their promise-laden prose, many personal finance publications and TV shows boil down to little more than touting lists of supposedly terrific investments. For example, after poring over one issue of a major financial magazine, I found that this publication had recommended explicitly or by implication (that is, it wrote about the investment in a glowing or otherwise positive way) some sixty-two stocks and mutual funds—that's sixty-two supposedly great deals in a single issue. At that rate, this monthly magazine would recommend more than seven hundred stocks and funds over the course of just one year. Now, really, what are you supposed to do, buy them all? And let's just say that you have enough time and money to do that—what do you do the next year? Sell last year's group and buy the seven hundred or so new recommendations the magazine makes, as if you were trading in last year's car model for this year's? Hold on to the first year's recommendations and buy next year's, too, so that in the space of just two years you have an investment portfolio bursting with 1,400 or more investments?

The problem is that many of the investments that are the darlings of the supposed experts one year flame out the next. So if most of your investment portfolio consists of stocks or funds recommended at the peak of their performance, I have three words of warning: Look out below! In this book you won't find lists of "the best" stocks or mutual funds. Instead you'll find cogent, easy-to-understand advice that will help you set a sane investment strategy and choose your own stocks and funds that can produce solid long-term returns.

Okay, enough about my investing approach and what this book will help you do. It's time to start soaking up my sage advice, practical tips, and spellbinding factoids. Before you go to chapter 1, though, spend a few minutes taking "The Financially Challenged Investing IQ Test" on the next page.

THE FINANCIALLY CHALLENGED INVESTING IQ TEST

I could tell you that you should take this quiz so we can establish a baseline for measuring the vast improvement in your financial knowledge after you've finished reading this book. But I know you won't fall for that line, so I won't even try it. No, the real reason to take the quiz is that it's fun, although there is always the risk you could learn something from it.

I have chosen the twenty questions below through a rigorous computerized screening process statistically valid to the fourteenth decimal place to gauge your investing acumen. Okay, a slight exaggeration. But these questions are definitely based on my encyclopedic knowledge of the financial world. All right, the truth is I came up with them off the top of my head. But I did write them on a computer. In any case, take the test so you can see how much you know—or don't know, as the case may be—about investing. Tips for scoring your performance follow the quiz.

Question #1: If a friend of yours told you he was making money buying and selling Ginnie and Fannie Maes, you would say:

a. "Gee, I thought that sort of thing was illegal in every state but Nevada."

b. "Great, I've always loved their candy."

c. "Careful, if interest rates go up, your investment will get hammered—and if rates come down, you may not do so hot, either."

Question #2: The S&P 500 is

a. that new version of the Indy 500 that's open only to investment bankers in pinstripe suits and red suspenders who drive Volvo 740 wagons.

b. the nickname for the Standard & Poor's 500—a commonly used benchmark to gauge the health of the stock market that's made up of the share prices of five hundred large U.S. corporations.

Question #3: What's the difference between armed robbery and stockbrokers peddling an investment that will pay them a fat commission?

a. Stockbrokers rarely wear stockings over their heads and put a gun in your face.

b. Armed robbers don't usually call you on the phone before they take your money.

c. Armed robbers work longer hours and don't get nearly the pension benefits brokers do.

d. Wait a minute . . . aside from the armed part, are you sure there's a difference?

Question #4: A muni bond is

a. the close relationship formed by Unification Church members during indoctrination sessions.

b. a type of bond issued by state and local governments that pays interest that is free from federal (and sometimes state and local) taxes to fund projects like building bridges and tunnels.

c. Same as b, except the real reason they're issued is so state and local officials can channel bond business to investment companies, which can in turn contribute big bucks to the officials' reelection campaigns.

Question #5: What is a 401(k)?

a. That thingamajig that comes right after a 401(j).

b. A tax-deferred savings plan your company sets up for you but never gets around to explaining exactly how it works or how you can use it most effectively.

Question #6: A DRIP is

a. a guy who carries his Texas Instruments scientific calculator in a plastic pocket saver.

b. a guy who carries a Texas Instruments scientific calculator, period.

c. a stock **d**ividend **re-i**nvestment **p**lan, which uses the dividends a company pays to buy extra shares of stock without charging you a commission.

Question #7: If a broker or financial planner tells you that he's a registered investment adviser, the proper response is

a. "I'm impressed—you must have met some pretty rigorous standards set by the Securities and Exchange Commission."

b. "You seem awfully young to have such an impressive title."

c. "Wait a minute. Can't anyone but a convicted felon pay the $150 registration fee and become a registered investment adviser?"

Question #8: An ADR is

a. a dyslexic offshoot of the Daughters of the American Revolution.

b. an American Depository Receipt, or a way to buy shares of foreign companies on a U.S. stock exchange rather than buying on a foreign bourse.

Question #9: If you believe in the random-walk theory, then you

a. never feel the need to consult a map.

b. get lost a lot.

c. believe that whether you pick stocks through laborious research or by throwing darts at the stock pages, you will wind up with about the same returns.

Question #10: What is a tender offer?

a. A marriage proposal made on bended knee to the sound of romantic music during a candlelight dinner.

b. An offer to buy the shares of a company that may precede a hostile takeover attempt.

Question #11: If an investment adviser told you he was thinking of covering his shorts, you would reply:

a. "Yes, and hurry—the BVD look just doesn't cut it in the office these days."

b. "What do you intend to cover them with—polka dots?"

c. "Don't you know that selling short is a risky strategy that can backfire and cost you big bucks?"

Question #12: A blind pool is

a. what you have when Stevie Wonder and Ray Charles shoot billiards.

b. a limited partnership or other offering that doesn't specify exactly how your money will be invested—in other words, trust us (you shouldn't).

Question #13: If a stockbroker called and offered you a chance to buy into an initial public offering (IPO), you would

a. run for your checkbook because IPOs are a great way for small investors to get in on the ground floor of some of the most exciting and profitable new stock issues.

b. immediately hang up because small investors often get fleeced in IPO deals.

c. ask the broker if IPO stands for "it's probably overpriced."

Question #14: A market correction is

a. any decline in stock prices of 10 percent or more.

b. a decline of 10 percent or more in stock prices that occurs just after you finally put some money into stocks or stock mutual funds.

c. I thought a and b always occurred at the same time.

Question #15: You're at a cocktail party when you overhear an attractive woman telling a friend she's considering naked options. Do you

a. quickly offer to give her a ride home?

b. tell her that great minds think alike—you're considering the same thing?

c. warn her that selling options on stocks she doesn't own can be the fast track to big losses in the stock market?

Question #16: If a broker, planner, or insurance agent told you that a variable annuity was a great way to rack up tax-deferred income and capital gains and that by eventually converting your variable account into a joint-and-survivor annuity you can assure a lifetime income for you and your spouse, you would say:

a. "Huh? Come again?"

b. "Wait a minute. Don't annuities hit you up the wazoo with stiff surrender penalties and steep annual fees that can virtually wipe out the tax advantages they offer?"

Question #17: A broker sells you a municipal bond that pays a very high rate of interest but has a call provision. The call provision means that

a. you have the right to call the broker back and ream him out if you lose money on the bond.

b. the broker has a right to call you any time he wants to try to sell you more bonds.

c. if interest rates drop, the bond issuer will probably swoop in and buy that high-rate bond back from you, forcing you to reinvest your money at lower rates of interest.

Question #18: Penny stocks are

a. stocks that sell for a low price, usually less than $5 a share.

b. stocks that sell for a low price, usually less than $5 a share, and are often sold by brokerage firms of dubious integrity.

c. stocks that people buy for several dollars a share but are lucky to get a penny for when they sell them.

Question #19: If an investment adviser confides in you that his investment strategy is based on "tactical asset allocation," you would say:

a. "Can you say that three times fast while eating a saltine cracker?"

b. "Isn't that just a fancy term for a losing strategy known as market timing?"

Question #20: If a stock market commentator says the market is reaching new highs but showing signs of poor breadth, that means

a. the Dow needs a shot of Listerine, pronto.

b. the commentator is a dentist-turned-stock market analyst.

c. the market averages are being driven to new heights by only a few large stocks, while the vast majority of smaller stocks are actually lagging behind.

The correct answers: What? You're taking this exercise seriously enough to want to check your answers and score yourself? Maybe you need more help than I thought. Okay, just for the record, here are the right answers. (Notice how in deference to today's liberal grading standards I accept multiple answers on several questions.) Question #1-c; #2-b; #3-a,b,c, or d; #4-b,c; #5-b; #6-c; #7-a, b, or c; #8-b; #9-c; #10-b; #11-c; #12-b; #13-b or c; #14-a; #15-c; #16-b; #17-c; #18-a, b, or c; #19-b; #20-c.

Figuring your score: Give yourself five points for each question you answered correctly. Here's an assessment of your abilities based on how you scored:

0–29: You're an investment disaster waiting to happen. Do not—repeat do *not*—sign any contracts or invest any money till you've read this book cover to cover.

30–49: Your knowledge level is typical of the average American—you know absolutely nothing. At this point it's dangerous for you even to talk to a broker or other financial adviser.

50–69: Congratulations! Since rigorous academic standards don't exist anymore, this score would probably be considered a passing grade today. But you're still ripe pickings for any unscrupulous adviser.

70–89: Gee, if I hadn't worded the questions so that the answers were so damn obvious, I might actually think you know something with a score like this. Don't fool yourself. If you went to the trouble to take this test and actually tote up your score, you're obviously no Peter Lynch or Warren Buffett (who, by the way, is *not* Jimmy Buffett's father).

90–100: Even I didn't score this high. You obviously cheated, which means you're in an acute state of denial and need to read this book immediately.

Flip the page and get started.

CHAPTER 1

The Deep, Dark Mysteries of Investing Revealed

• • • • • • • • • • •

Exposing Wall Street's Most Closely Guarded Secret

Okay, I want your undivided attention now because I'm about to reveal a secret that could put hundreds of thousands of stockbrokers, money managers, investment planners, and financial journalists out of business. Ready? Psst! Investing is actually pretty damn easy. We're not talking brain surgery here. The basic principles and strategies you must master to invest successfully are embarrassingly simple. Which is probably why investment professionals spend so much time trying to make the investing process seem more complicated than it is.

Think about it: you really have only two big decisions to make. The first is how you should divvy up your money among the three main classes of investment assets: stock funds (or individual stocks), bond funds (or individual bonds), and cash (essentially money-market funds, though bank accounts and short-term certificates of deposit would also qualify). The answer to that one is determined largely by how much you can tolerate seeing the value of your investment portfolio drop over the short term if the stock or bond market falls apart and how long you plan to keep your money invested before you start tapping your investment accounts for cash. The longer your money will be invested, the more you should tilt your mix toward stocks. The shorter the time period, the more toward bonds. Not exactly rocket science.

The second big decision is what specific stock funds (or individual stocks), bond funds (or individual bonds), and cash investments (money-market funds) you buy once you've determined the answer to question number one.

With more than 5,000 stock funds, 3,700 bond funds, and 1,100 money-market funds to choose from—not to mention thousands of individual stocks and bonds—this question may seem complicated. But the beauty of investing is that you don't have to pick the absolute best ones to succeed. Fact is, "pretty good" is a plenty high enough standard when it comes to picking investments. And average ain't bad, either. Consider this: If at the beginning of 1980 you had invested $10,000 in a stock mutual fund that earned just the *average* return for all funds that invest in a broad range of U.S. stocks, by late September 1998 your ten grand would have grown (before taxes) to just over $140,000. That translates to an average annual return of about 14.3 percent. Most people would—and should—be happy to settle for those kinds of numbers.

So if investing is so easy, you may ask, why do so many people screw it up? That brings us to another little-known fact about investing: What stands between most of us and investing success isn't our inability to master the principles of investing; it's our inability to master ourselves, by which I mean the emotions, mental lapses, and psychological quirks that often subvert our thinking process and make us do dumb things. In short, it's *our* behavior as much as the financial market's that ultimately determines whether we make or lose money over the long run. Don't believe me? Read on.

STOP LOOKING AT THE MARKET AND START LOOKING INSIDE YOURSELF

For years economists assumed that whether we were choosing a car or picking stocks or funds, we acted in a perfectly rational manner. That is, we gathered information and, with our brains whirring away like Pentium processors, arrived at a consistent and logical choice. To everyone but economists, this was obviously not true. Evidence abounds that we make all sorts of illogical and inconsistent decisions. People who claim to like music buy Michael Bolton albums. We not only elect politicians who later prove themselves to be of dubious integrity, but we reelect them. With a few notable exceptions, however, most of us don't make boneheaded decisions because we're dumb, we make them because a variety of mental and emotional quirks we never think about screw up our thought processes.

In recent years a number of economists, psychologists, and other researchers have begun to explore the way our brains work when we grapple with questions like investing. The result is an emerging academic discipline called *psychoeconomics*. Not to be confused with economics for psychos, psychoeconomics attempts to shed light on the irrational psychological tendencies and predilections that can lead us to make lousy decisions. I'm not going to claim that by understanding your emotional and psychological peccadilloes you'll be able to rid yourself of them and always make logical, clearheaded choices. But if you at least know a bit about how subconscious impulses might lead you awry, you stand a better chance of guarding against the errors in judgment they help cause. In this section I've outlined four common psychological mistakes or traps that we can all fall prey to:

THE FRAIDY-CAT SYNDROME: Psychologists and economists who study individuals' behavior when weighing financial alternatives have found that most of us experience about twice as much pain from losses as we do pleasure from gains. In other words, we fear losing 10 percent on an investment twice as much as we look forward to gaining 10 percent. At the same time, most people, even when they're investing money for long-term goals, tend to check the results on their investments frequently, sometimes as much as weekly or even daily. Put these two tendencies together, and you get a phenomenon that Schlomo Benartzi of the University of California and University of Chicago's Richard Thaler call *myopic loss aversion*—loosely translated as being overly concerned with short-term setbacks. Benartzi and Thaler hypothesize that investors' fear of short-term losses may sabotage their long-term investment strategy by leading them to put too little of their money in stocks, which are prone to many short-term setbacks but nonetheless have the highest long-term returns. The idea is that our shortsightedness, so to speak, about losses prevents us from focusing on stocks' ability to generate superior long-term gains and makes us pay too much attention to the temporary dips in market prices.

THE OVERCONFIDENCE TRAP: It's amazing how quickly we can go from feeling we know very little about investing to the certainty that we've got it mastered. But psychologists and behavioral economists have found that in many cases our investing mistakes are caused from our own overconfidence, especially when we believe we have information that gives us special insight, such as a hot tip from a friend or supposed expert. This feeling that we really know what we're talking about also arises when we're considering investing in a company we're familiar with or whose products or services we use. Investment publications help foster this notion by supplying us with accounts of superstar investors like Peter Lynch, who supposedly invested in Dunkin' Donuts after he found he liked its coffee. (Of course, Lynch no doubt did tons of research on the company as well before he went from Dunkin' Donuts java to its stock.) But familiarity doesn't necessarily breed great stock picks. By investing in companies we know, we may be doing little more than satisfying an underlying need to feel comfortable about where we invest our cash.

For example, after examining the stock-ownership records of all seven of the Baby Bells (the regional Bell operating companies that resulted after AT&T was split up), Columbia University professor Gur Huberman found that in all but one state (Montana) more people hold shares of their local Baby Bell than any of the other six. What's more, in forty-four states the amount of money invested in the local Bells exceeded the average amount invested in "outsider" Bells by a margin of more than three to one. Presumably the investors in each state bought their local Bell because they believed it was a better investment than the other Bells; otherwise why would they have chosen the local company? But all these investors can't be right; every local Bell can't be a better investment than the other six. What is probably at work here is the notion that investors who live in a particular state feel they know more about the companies in their area. This notion also probably explains why Apple Computer fans might be more likely to invest in Apple than Microsoft, or people who've had good luck with Whirlpool appliances might be inclined to buy Whirlpool stock.

THE HERD MENTALITY MIND-SET: If you're at a cocktail party and during the evening three different people mention a terrific mutual fund they've invested in, would you be tempted to buy it yourself?

If you're like most people, you probably would, because researchers have found that we tend to invest with a herd mentality—that is, we often abdicate our independent judgment and instead rely heavily on the advice, opinions, and actions of others. Not even professional investors are immune to acting like sheep; indeed, they may be even more prone to it than novices. Finance professors Josef Lakonishok, Andrei Shleifer, and Robert Vishny have theorized that one of the reasons fund managers lag the S&P 500 so badly may be because they gravitate toward "glamour stocks"—that is, shares are already so popular with investors that they tend to be overpriced. So why would managers buy stocks that would seem to have limited potential for outsize gains? Well, the profs hypothesize that the managers may feel they'll have an easier time rationalizing mediocre performance as long as they stick to stocks that no one would ever doubt are good companies.

Problem is, the more you're willing to follow the crowd, the more likely you are to get swept up in investment fads that have little chance for long-term success, and the greater your chances of buying a hot stock or fund *du jour* that might be a flash in the pan.

THE CRYSTAL BALL PITFALL: This foible probably wreaks the most havoc with investors' money. Investors have a knack for assuming that recent trends will continue indefinitely into the future. When an investment has had a phenomenal year, as gold funds did when they soared to average 90 percent gains in 1993, many investors see that as a sign to put their money into a winner. Indeed, that's why the funds that get high ratings from fund-tracking firms like Morningstar tend to attract the most cash flow from individual investors. The same goes for stocks. The prices of stocks of companies that have posted rapidly growing profits often get bid up to ever higher prices because investors believe the company will keep churning out those earnings in the future just as it has in the past. In fact, there's little, if any, evidence that the mutual funds that came out on top in the past will continue to do so in the future. After their spectacular returns in 1993, for example, gold funds lost 12 percent in 1994, gained a modest 3 percent and 8 percent the next two years, and then dropped 43 percent in 1997. Sizzle can turn to fizzle pretty quickly on Wall Street.

A LOOK INSIDE
AN INVESTOR'S BRAIN

In the following illustration, you get a rare chance to peek inside the typical investor's brain and see why our thought process is often so screwed up when it comes to investing. Notice the struggle that's going on between the conservative half—the one that hates risk and is always looking for more safety—and the aggressive half—the cocky side that's oblivious of risk and is always pushing for bigger gains. Some investors manage to prevent either side from getting the upper hand. These are the people who buy and hold for the long term, favor index mutual funds, and generally try to keep investing costs to a minimum.

But for many people one sphere holds sway. When the conservative side rules, investors cower in money funds and bank certificates of deposit (CDs). Investors with a dominant aggressive side, on the other hand, load up on overpriced Internet stocks, invest in the funds with the highest recent returns, and hang out in Internet chat sessions, hoping to pick up hot stock tips. In extreme cases the aggressive half of the brain takes over. These people become online day traders and, if not treated, eventually may become option or commodities brokers.

THE TYPICAL INVESTOR'S BRAIN

CONSERVATIVE SIDE   AGGRESSIVE SIDE

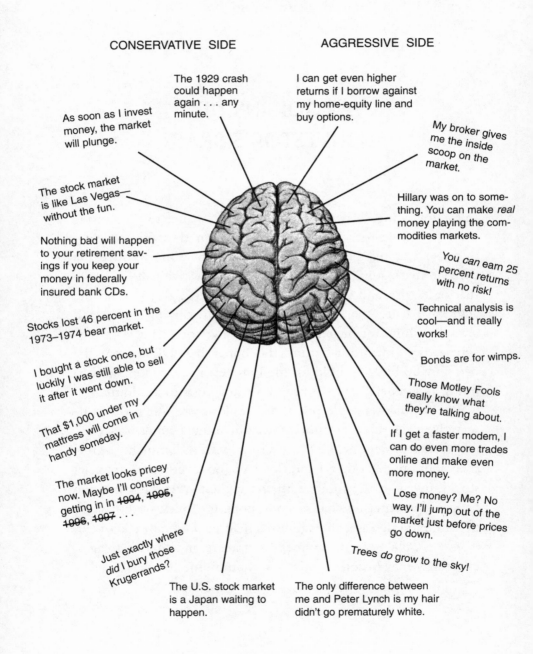

The 1929 crash could happen again . . . any minute.

I can get even higher returns if I borrow against my home-equity line and buy options.

As soon as I invest money, the market will plunge.

My broker gives me the inside scoop on the market.

The stock market is like Las Vegas without the fun.

Hillary was on to something. You can make *real* money playing the commodities markets.

Nothing bad will happen to your retirement savings if you keep your money in federally insured bank CDs.

You *can* earn 25 percent returns with no risk!

Stocks lost 46 percent in the 1973–1974 bear market.

Technical analysis is cool—and it really works!

I bought a stock once, but luckily I was still able to sell it after it went down.

Bonds are for wimps.

That $1,000 under my mattress will come in handy someday.

Those Motley Fools really know what they're talking about.

The market looks pricey now. Maybe I'll consider getting in in ~~1994~~, ~~1995~~, ~~1996~~, ~~1997~~ . . .

If I get a faster modem, I can do even more trades online and make even more money.

Lose money? Me? No way. I'll jump out of the market just before prices go down.

Just exactly where did I bury those Krugerrands?

Trees *do* grow to the sky!

The U.S. stock market is a Japan waiting to happen.

The only difference between me and Peter Lynch is my hair didn't go prematurely white.

Now that we're aware of all those self-defeating habits lurking deep in our subconscious, we can move on to my handy list of investing tips, a road map if you will, for the investing journey you're about to embark on. These points lay out the broad guidelines for the overall investing approach I advocate—namely, taking advantage of the long-term returns the financial markets offer patient investors while avoiding fancy and expensive strategies that benefit investment salesmen more than you.

TOP TEN INVESTING TIPS FOR THE FINANCIALLY CHALLENGED

1. DON'T EVEN *THINK* OF TRYING TO OUTSMART THE MARKET. One of the biggest con jobs perpetrated on the investing public by Wall Street firms and many investment magazines and newsletters is the notion that well-informed investors (in other words, the ones who listen to Wall Street firms and read these publications) can boost their profits by loading up on stocks just before the market stampedes to new highs and dumping them before stock prices stumble. Of course, no respectable firm or magazine comes right out and advocates the largely discredited practice known as *market timing*—that is, switching *all* of your money out of stocks and into a safe haven like a CD or money-market fund if the market looks as though it's about to tank, or doing the opposite if stock prices appear ready to soar. Instead they resort to a kind of modified market timing that's cloaked in coded phrases. For example, an investment guru on a TV financial talk show might suggest that it's time "to lighten up on stocks" because "the market looks overpriced." Or a magazine may recommend that you "take profits in some of your winners" because the market is "ready to stall" or "headed for a setback." Read between the lines, though, and what they're really saying is that it's possible to forecast the future of the market—and that you can take steps in advance to capitalize on it.

Unfortunately no one's crystal ball is clear enough to make such forecasts accurately. First of all, just predicting when the market will plunge is difficult enough. After the stock market charged to 31 percent gains in 1995, for example, many market prognosticators averred that 1996 would be a lousy year because outsize returns are often followed by lackluster gains or losses. Of course, 1996's gains of 23 percent threw cold water on that theory. And although some investors were certainly worried about how much higher stock prices could go after the Dow Jones Industrial Average broke above the 9,300 level in July 1998, the overwhelming majority of investors were still caught off guard when the Dow dropped almost 20 percent over the next month or so.

But let's say that someone is smart or lucky enough to foretell market setbacks. Question is, can that same guru also tell you when to get back into the market? Not likely. The fact is, when the market rebounds, it often does so swiftly, scoring much of its gains in just a few days. Miss those days, and you miss those gains. To paraphrase the New York Lotto slogan: You gotta be in it to win it.

To get an idea of just how much you would risk by jumping in and out of the market, consider this: If you had invested $1,000 in stocks in 1963 and sat tight over the next thirty years, your one grand would have snowballed to $32,000, a bit more than a 12 percent annual return. But if you had missed only the ten best days for the stock market during that period, your return would have dropped to 10.5 percent, and your $1,000 would be worth $20,000—not bad, but quite a bit to give up for missing just ten days over thirty years. And if you missed the ninety best days, your return would have fallen to a measly 3.3 percent, and your one grand would be worth just $2,700, or less than the

$6,380 you would have earned had you just kept it in a money-market fund.

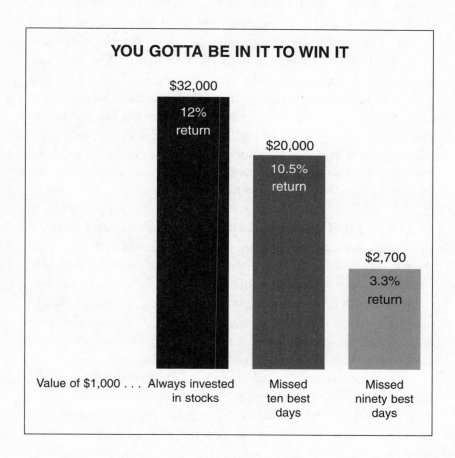

YOU GOTTA BE IN IT TO WIN IT

$32,000

12% return

$20,000

10.5% return

$2,700

3.3% return

Value of $1,000 . . . Always invested in stocks — Missed ten best days — Missed ninety best days

All right, so you're convinced that once you're in, you'll hang in for the long haul. But perhaps you're still worried about *when* to get in. Maybe you have an inherently lousy sense of timing; you sank $10,000 into Beta videocassette equipment in the 1980s. You just *know* that the minute you stick a few bucks into stocks or stock mutual funds, word will spread that the last sucker is in—and the Dow will drop off a ten thousand-point cliff.

Well, I've got some information that will help take the edge off your paranoia. Mutual fund firm T. Rowe Price decided to look at what would have happened had a hypothetical investor plowed $2,000 into stocks each year for the twenty years through 1996 *and had the incredibly bad luck to make each investment on the worst possible day of the year—that is, the day the market was at its yearly high.* So how did this sad sack do? Not bad. The $40,000 this hapless investor stashed into stocks turned into $223,135 for an annualized return of 10.3 percent. Moral: Time can make up for bad timing. Think time *in* the market, not tim*ing* the market. The longer you stay invested in the stock market, the better your chances of making money. Hang in there long enough, and you might make enough dough to add to your collection of rare Beta videocassettes.

2. TUNE OUT THE NOISE. Access to up-to-date financial news and investing information used to be limited to pros who worked on Wall Street. But with the advent of mutual funds, personal finance publications, cable TV, and the Internet, you're virtually inundated with the latest stats, breaking news, and instant analysis. You can even sign up for free e-mail alerts with the latest news and price updates on as many as two hundred stocks or mutual funds.

So if information is power, individual investors today must be more powerful than ever before, right? Not quite.

Unfortunately it's impossible to tell in advance what kind of an effect, if any, the "big news" everyone is talking about will have on your investments even in the short term, let alone over longer periods. In the case of the turmoil in Asian stock markets in October 1997, for example, jitters in the Hong Kong market did help send the Dow down 554 points in one day. Of course, the next day the U.S. market rallied 337 points, and ultimately the Dow finished the year with a 24.8 percent gain.

THE PARADOX OF VIGILANCE

You might figure that investors who pay the most attention to financial news would automatically earn higher returns than their more lackadaisical counterparts who don't follow the latest news about the market. And you would be wrong. Why? Because of what I call *the paradox of vigilance.*

Although it may seem counterintuitive, it appears that following the financial news can actually hurt your returns. The 1980s Harvard University psychologist Paul Andreassen performed experiments in which one group of people bought or sold stocks based only on recent share prices, while a second group traded after receiving price information plus news headlines about the stocks. The result: when stock prices were volatile, the investors who read the headlines earned *less than half* the returns of the investors who suffered a news blackout, so to speak.

Why would no news be good news? The reason is probably because people have a tendency to take news as a prediction about a stock's future. If a drop in the price of a stock is accompanied by bad news—earnings are down—investors are likely to expect the negative trend to continue. So they unload the stock. If a price increase comes with good news—earnings are up—investors may take this as a sign to buy a stock. Since thousands of investors may be reacting this way, a stock can be driven to unrealistically high prices on good news or unrealistically low levels on bad news. That means someone buying on good news may wind up paying an inflated price, while an investor who sells on bad news might be getting less than the stock's true worth.

My advice: Feel free to follow the news about your investments if you're sure that doing so won't compel you to take action. But if scanning the financial pages every day or flipping through the cable TV shows gives you a craving to fool around with your investments, then I suggest you take an approach the late pyschedelic guru Timothy Leary might have tried: Turn off the TV, tune out the financial pages, and drop out of the mind-set that you can boost your returns by reacting to the daily news.

I'm not advocating that you yank your cable TV connection or cancel your subscription to *The Wall Street Journal*. It's important to keep informed about the progress (or lack of it) of the market and your specific investments. But I do advise that your first reaction to any news event should be, *Do nothing*. That's right: Don't just do something, stand there! Then take your time to analyze coolly and rationally what has happened. Can you really tell what the future effect of this event will be? If the news represents some fundamental change about an investment—say, the chief financial officer of that hot new company your broker recommended has just been indicted for cooking the firm's books—then you may want to act on the information. Even then you should do so only after doing more research. (The company's long-term prospects could still be sound despite the malfeasance.) But most news doesn't give you much of an insight into the future. Which means you should listen and absorb it, but rarely—and I mean almost never—act on it immediately. And that especially holds true for specific investments some financial poo-bah recommends on radio, TV, in a publication, or online. By the time the news is getting to you, chances are much of the easy money has been made and all you're doing is providing the profit for someone who invested before the investment was touted in print, on the air, or on the Net.

3. CRACK DOWN ON COSTS. Most investors pay a lot of attention to the returns they earn from investments but think little about the costs of investing. In fact, you have a lot more control over expenses like the brokerage commissions you generate and the amount of fees you pay to invest in mutual funds than you do over the future returns the stock and bond markets are likely to dole out. And make no mistake about it: every cent you pay in commissions and fees reduces your returns—not just by the amount of the expense itself, but by what you could have earned if the money you shelled out in fees had also been invested.

Here's a quick example of how bloated expenses can erode your gains in mutual funds. Let's say, for example, that your neighbor invests $10,000 in a stock fund that was sold to him by a broker or financial planner and that has a sales load (that is, a sales commission) of 5.75 percent and ongoing annual expenses of 1.5 percent of assets, while you buy a no-load stock fund directly from the mutual fund company that has annual expenses of 0.75 percent. And let's further assume that both funds earn 10 percent *before* expenses for the next twenty years.

So how did you both do? Well, since 5.75 percent of your neighbor's ten grand was siphoned off the top in a sales commission, he actually invested $9,425, which earned a net return of 8.5 percent a year (10 percent gross return minus 1.5 percent in expenses). After twenty years he ended up with $48,181 (before taxes). You, on the other hand, invested your entire $10,000 and earned 9.25 percent annually (10 percent minus 0.75 percent), giving you a total of $58,672 after twenty years (also before taxes). So in this case, at least, the investor who choose the lower-cost alternative gained an extra $10,491. Not bad for one $10,000 investment.

Now, to be fair, I have to admit that the $575 commission your neighbor paid to the broker or planner who sold him the fund might have been worthwhile. Without the broker or planner's help, your neighbor's ten grand might have languished in a bank CD or a savings account, earning a paltry 3 percent to 6 percent. Furthermore, I've assumed that both investments had the same annual gain before expenses. It's possible that your neighbor's fund might have earned more than enough to make up for its higher expenses. If, for example, his fund had gained 10 percent annually after expenses, your neighbor would have $63,407, or $4,735 more than you. Possible? Sure, but to get 10 percent after taxes, your neighbor's fund would have had to earn 11.5 percent annually before taxes, or a full 1.5 percentage points more than your fund. Is a fund manager likely to earn an extra 1.5 percentage points a year for twenty years without taking on lots more risk? I don't think so, because there's no evidence that funds with higher expenses are likely to outperform funds with low expenses. In fact, if anything, the opposite appears to be true.

4. TAKE THE EMOTION OUT OF INVESTING. I think that most of us start out with the idea of taking a rigorous, disciplined approach to investing. But somewhere along the way we get sidetracked and give in to emotional impulses (though we usually lay a thin veneer of rationalization over our emotional decisions to give us a bit of intellectual cover).

As long as your emotions dominate your intellect, you're likely to lurch from one hot investment to another—and end up with withering losses. My suggestion: Bench your emotions; just take them out of the game. The most effective way to do that is to invest on a regular basis by following a strategy known as *dollar-cost averaging.* You invest a certain amount each month—say, $100—in stocks or mutual funds. And you put that hundred in each month, regardless of what the market is doing. When the stock market is rising, your $100 buys fewer shares of your stocks or funds; when prices fall, you get more shares for your money. This technique won't protect you from stock market losses; if the market falls, the value of your holdings will drop—although the next $100 that goes in will pick up more shares than before. But dollar-cost averaging will prevent you from giving way to your emotions and plowing most of your money into stocks after prices have skyrocketed. And it will force you to buy after the market has dropped, when stocks are usually a better buy but when many investors are too nervous to scoop them up. This technique generally works better with mutual funds than with stocks, because trading commissions can eat up too much of a small investment like $100, but you can also dollar-cost average with stocks by sticking to direct purchase plans.

To give you an idea of how dollar-cost averaging can pay off over many years, consider this: If you had invested $100 a month in the Vanguard Index 500 fund—a stock fund that buys the large-company stocks that make up the Standard & Poor's 500—starting in January 1978, you would have had an account worth $174,230 (before taxes) by the end of December 1997. True, the stock market's returns during this period were nothing short of phenomenal, and there's no guarantee we'll see such a runup again. What's more, even during this period there were times when your account balance would have declined. For example, between August 1987 and January 1988—a period that includes the October 1987 crash—your account balance would have dropped 22 percent. Similarly, you would have gotten clawed by the brief bear market of the summer and fall of 1990, driving the balance down 30 percent in November 1990.

But if you had held on during those downturns—and continued plopping a hundred bucks into the fund each and every month—then you would have effectively turned $24,000 of principal into a pile worth $174,230. No fancy strategies or arcane techniques. Just persistence and letting the general long-term trend in stock-price appreciation work for you.

5. SPREAD YOUR DOUGH AROUND. If you somehow knew in advance the names of, say, the ten stocks that were absolutely, positively, without a doubt going to skyrocket to the biggest gains over the next year or so, and you also by some stroke of genius (or more probably luck) knew the names of the ten stocks that were equally certain to flame out with horrible losses, you would buy the rockets, not the crash-and-burners, right?

Unfortunately, neither you nor Wall Street's army of securities analysts, portfolio strategists, and other soothsayers can make those kinds of predictions in advance with a high degree of accuracy. I mean, on a year-to-year basis forecasters aren't even able to make accurate broader predictions—like whether stocks will outperform bonds—let alone pinpoint exactly which of the more than eight thousand or so publicly traded stocks in the United States will be the best performers.

So how do you handle that frustrating inability to see into the future? You rely on the two most fundamental principles of rational investing: *diversification* and *asset allocation*. Although the two are sometimes used interchangeably, technically there is a slight difference between the two concepts.

Diversification refers to buying a broad range of a particular type of investment. Instead of buying just one stock, you buy ten to twenty stocks of different companies in different industries. That way, if your assessment about one or two companies is wrong—or even if it's essentially right, but something goes wrong that you could neither foresee nor control—your entire wad won't be devastated. Diversification does *not,* however, protect you from market downturns. If the entire stock market goes down, your stocks will most likely get hurt, too.

Asset allocation also involves diversifying, but instead of buying a broad range of a single type of investment, you spread your money across different types of assets, typically stocks, bonds, and cash. (Cash in this sense means incredibly stable investments like money-market funds or Treasury bills.) The idea is that since these investments don't all move up and down in synch with each other, one part of your portfolio can be churning out gains while another part is heading south.

So owning some of all three asset classes—stocks, bonds, and cash—prevents the value of your investment stash from being obliterated if, say, the stock market heads south or bond prices crash because investors suddenly fear that inflation is making a comeback. Some people who've heard of the concept of asset allocation think it immunizes their portfolio against losses. Not so. For example, when stock prices dropped 21.5 percent during the big market meltdown in October 1987, government bonds actually gained 6.2 percent. So if you had had, say, 60 percent of your money in stocks and 40 percent in bonds, your portfolio still would have lost money during the October 1987 crash, but your overall loss for that month would have been 10.4 percent, or less than half the 21.5 percent you would have lost in an all-stock portfolio. In chapter 7 we'll go into more detail about how to build a portfolio of investments that can help you achieve your goals with an acceptable level of risk.

6. LAP UP GOVERNMENT AND CORPORATE FREEBIES LIKE 401(K)S AND IRAS. Do you have so much money that you can afford to throw away tens of thousands of dollars? I know I don't. But chucking away money is exactly what you're doing if your investing strategy doesn't include maxing out on tax-advantaged retirement savings plans like a 401(k) or an individual retirement account (IRA).

Basically you get three big perks by participating in a 401(k) plan. First, an immediate tax break: The money you contribute to a 401(k) plan isn't counted as taxable income. So if you are in the 28 percent federal tax bracket and put $4,000 a year into a 401(k), you shave your tax bill by $1,120 each year. Depending on how you look at it, that $1,120 is more money for you to invest outside your 401(k) or to spend on necessities or frivolities—or you could think of it as the IRS picking up $1,120 of your $4,000 401(k) contribution.

Next, you get valuable tax deferral: The principal and earnings in your account grow free of taxes until you pull them out. So instead of having to watch the taxman siphon off some of your profits each year, you can reinvest every cent you earn in your account, which will allow you to earn profits on your profits and boost your rate of return. One downside: *All* withdrawals from 401(k) accounts (as well as IRAs) are taxed at ordinary income rates, which can run as high as 39.6 percent. Even long-term capital gains that would normally qualify for the maximum capital gains rate of 20 percent are taxed at ordinary income rates. But if you're investing for many years, the benefit of tax deferral should overcome this disadvantage.

The final bennie: Most people in 401(k) plans also qualify for matching contributions from the company sponsoring the plan. Typically, companies allow employees to put 6 percent to 10 percent of their salary into the 401(k)—the government also sets a maximum contribution, $10,000 in 1998, which is adjusted for inflation—and usually match half of the first 6 percent, thus kicking in 3 percent of your salary. Some employers are more generous, others less.

Add up these benefits, and you come away with some pretty impressive numbers. If you earn $50,000 a year and your company's 401(k) plan allows you to stick 6 percent of your salary into the plan—and your employer kicked in half of what you contribute—you would sock away a total of $4,500 a year ($3,000 from you plus $1,500 from your employer), plus enjoy tax savings, assuming you're in the 28 percent tax bracket, of $840 annually (28 percent of $3,000). In other words, after figuring in $840 in tax savings, plus a $1,500 company match, your employer and Uncle Sam would effectively be footing $2,340 of your $4,500 401(k) contribution, *or more than half of it!* With that kind of head start—putting up just $2,160 and getting to invest $4,500—you obviously don't have to be an investing genius to see the benefits of participating in a 401(k).

You may also be able to cash in on the tax advantages of one of several types of IRAs, depending on such factors as your age, income, and whether you're covered by an employer's retirement plan. For example, you may be able to put up to $2,000 a year into an IRA and deduct that two grand from your taxable income—a savings of $560 for someone in the 28 percent tax bracket. Your contribution and earnings would compound without the drag of taxes, until you withdraw the money. If you don't qualify for a deductible IRA, you can put $2,000 into a nondeductible IRA, where your money will at least grow tax-deferred until you pull it out. Or you may qualify for the new Roth IRA that Congress created in 1997. Your contribution to a Roth isn't tax-deductible, but you can pull your money out *tax-free* after age 59½, as long as you've had your Roth account at least five years. One thing you can't do, unfortunately, is put $2,000 in each type of IRA every year. Your total IRA contribution can't exceed $2,000 in any year.

Figuring out which combination of 401(k) and IRA accounts is best for you can be a real mind bender because of the numerous variables involved—your income, age, present and likely future tax rates, and how long you plan to invest. It almost always pays to put away as much as you can into your 401(k) plan, or at the very least to invest enough to get the maximum employer match. As for IRAs, the Roth is usually the best deal if you don't expect your tax rate to decline in retirement; otherwise a deductible IRA is generally the better choice. You can get some help in determining which type of IRA is best for you by going to Vanguard's Web site (www.vanguard.com) or buying the CD-ROM or diskette version of T. Rowe Price's IRA Analyzer (800-333-0740). Both of these sources can also help you with the even more difficult question of whether to convert existing IRAs to Roth accounts.

7. DON'T BE XENOPHOBIC—BUY FOREIGN. When it comes to investing, most Americans feel there's no place like home. Studies show that only 20 percent to 30 percent of U.S. investors ever invest in foreign securities. That isolationist approach is understandable, given some of the havoc we've witnessed in recent years in bourses around the world.

But if you are willing to add to your portfolio a dollop of mutual funds that invest in foreign shares, you stand a good chance of picking up a few nifty benefits. First, you'll get a shot at superior returns. True, lots of foreign markets have crashed and burned recently, as I just noted, and yes, U.S. stocks have delivered larger gains than foreign shares overall for much of the 1990s. But if the U.S. market cools off, foreign markets could begin to look better again compared with the U.S. market.

The other perk foreign securities offer is that they can actually dampen the overall volatility of your investment portfolio—that is, they can help limit the ups and downs in the value of your holdings. The idea that foreign stocks could make your portfolio less jumpy probably seems absurd given the swan dives many foreign stock markets have taken in recent years and considering that in 1997 trouble in Asian markets also helped drive down the price of U.S. shares. But while the U.S. and foreign economies are increasingly linked and our markets and overseas exchanges sometimes go down together during a major crisis, over longer periods of time U.S. and foreign share prices tend to move in different cycles. So keeping, say, 25 percent of your stock or stock mutual fund holdings in one or two international funds could reduce the fluctuations in your portfolio by 5 percent to 10 percent.

8. DEVELOP A SKEPTICAL ATTITUDE. Someone could make a fortune—and do investors a big favor—by inventing the investment equivalent of a Geiger counter. We could call it "the financial b.s. detector." I'm thinking of a pocket-size gizmo you would point at brokers, financial planners, and other investment salespeople while they're doing their sales spiel that would emit a piercing cry or message (*Aaaaooogah, aaaooogah. This sounds suspicious. Hold on to your checkbook! Do not give this person your money!*) whenever the product they're pitching is in any way bogus or the returns or strategies they're touting are unrealistic.

Until such a handy gadget comes along, however, you should work on developing a sixth sense to protect yourself from the inevitable array of investment sales pitches. The best defense: Demand plenty of information, such as a prospectus and performance data, before putting your money into any investment—and ask that the person selling you the investment disclose how and how much he or she is being paid in commissions or other fees.

9. KEEP IT SIMPLE. If I had the power to banish for all time just two words from the world of investing, it would probably be this pair: "sophisticated investing." Why? Because I believe that more harm is done by brokers, financial planners, personal finance magazines, and other peddlers of investment advice in the name of so-called sophisticated investing than all the out-right scams and bunko schemes combined. In the name of sophisticated investing, people have been sucked into the most outrageous investments over the years: speculative small-company stocks, bond funds with risky derivatives, limited part-nerships for everything from commercial real estate to rare coins to jojoba bean plantations, high-risk commodity funds, shares of windmill farms, and stakes in high-risk oil-drilling operations, to name just a few. Stockbrokers thrive on the pitch that they're introducing you to the exclusive world of high finance, where the "smart money" makes the "serious bucks." What they're often offering you is a chance to invest in the stock of a new, untested company that their firm may own a piece of. Invest-ment newsletters often push market-timing or index-trading schemes that purport to beat the market with low levels of risk.

In my experience, the more "sophisticated" an investment is, the bigger the fee it pays the person hawking it, and the more likely the thing is to blow up on you. You can get by quite well without loading up on gold or platinum futures or S&P 100 index options. You needn't feel you've missed out on an oppor-tunity of a lifetime if you never sell a stock short (a strategy that involves borrowing a stock whose price you think will fall, selling it, and then replacing it later at a cheaper price for a profit—if you're lucky). So the next time a broker or planner tells you you're ready to move up to some "sophisticated investing" and that he's got just the right opportunity for you, tell him you're too smart to want to be a sophisticated investor, so he'll have to find another pigeon.

10. ADOPT THE NIKE APPROACH TO INVESTING: JUST DO IT! If you remember just three words of advice from this entire book, let it be this trio: Start investing early. Don't pro-crastinate. Just do it. Sure, you can always find a reason to stall. Maybe the market's been charging to record highs lately, and you fear it's about to come crashing back to earth. Perhaps stock prices have already begun to ratchet downward, and you're afraid we're on the verge of a long bear market. Whatever your excuse is, forget it. The sooner you begin salting money away, the longer you can enjoy the wonder of compounding gains—that is, watching the money you start with generate gains that, in turn, produce more gains, which lead to even more, and so on. What's more, the earlier you start, the more time you have to make up for any mistakes you might make along the way.

Just how big an advantage does an early start give you? Let's assume you have a friend the same age as you who's a real early bird, someone who gets a jump on everything she does. This person begins investing $5,000 a year at age thirty-five and continues that regimen until she's forty-five. After that she doesn't invest any new money but keeps her original capital of $50,000 ($5,000 a year for ten years), plus all the gains it generated, invested until she's sixty-five. You, on the other hand, are a bit of a procrastinator who doesn't begin investing $5,000 a year until ten years later, when you're forty-five. You also sock away your five grand for ten years and then let your stash remain invested until you're sixty-five. Since you're both rational, intelligent adults, let's assume you both earn a reasonable 10 percent annual return. (And for simplicity's sake, let's leave taxes out of this example.)

Okay, so you've both invested diligently and earned the same rate of return. The only difference: Your friend got a ten-year head start. So where do you both stand at age sixty-five? Well, you would have a stash worth about $227,350—not bad for putting money away for ten years and letting it sit. But your pile of money is a pittance compared with that of your early bird friend, who is sitting on a nest egg of roughly $589,700. That's right, her jump on you has given her $362,350 more than you have. I call that difference the price of procrastination. It's her reward for digging in early and your penalty for starting late.

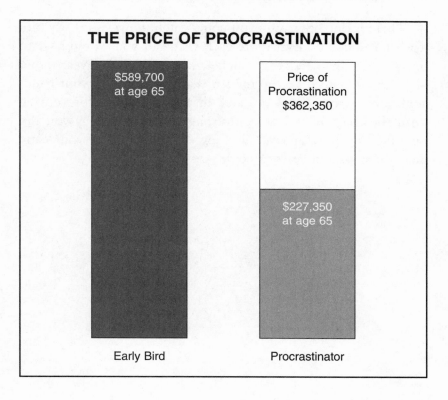

THE PRICE OF PROCRASTINATION

$589,700 at age 65

Price of Procrastination $362,350

$227,350 at age 65

Early Bird

Procrastinator

Oh, but maybe you think that this example doesn't really apply to you. After all, with the superior investing skills you'll get from reading this book, you will be able to close the gap by earning a higher rate of return, right? Tempted as I am to go along with that rationale for my own self-serving reasons, I know that your chances of earning returns lofty enough to compensate for ten years of dillydallying run somewhere between zero and zilch. In fact, you would have to earn a return of roughly 16.5 percent a year for each of the ten years that you invest $5,000, then earn that same 16.5 percent return for the next ten years. In short, you would have to grab average annual gains of 16.5 percent for two decades. That's a 40 percent to 60 percent higher return than the stock market typically averages over the long run. I wouldn't count on it.

There is one other way you could catch up to your early bird friend. You could invest more each year. But you would have to invest more than twice as much—almost $13,000 a year rather than $5,000—to make up for ten years of sitting on your hands and your money. So why make things any harder for yourself than they have to be? Start investing whatever money you can scrounge up now, and you'll enjoy the dividends of your early start for years and years to come.

CHAPTER 2

How to (Legally) Find the Money to Invest

• • • • • • • • • • •

Don't Even *Think* of Investing Until You've Become a Steady Saver

Yoù've probably heard of those Zen masters who achieve spiritual nirvana by sitting on a mountaintop and pondering profound concepts like the sound of one hand clapping. Well, the financial equivalent of that mental-philosophical-religious exercise would be trying to envision how much wealth you would create by investing without saving regularly.

Let me save you the intellectual trouble: Unless you start saving early and do it often, you won't accumulate any real wealth to speak of. Except for those few of us who are fortunate enough to start life with a large trust fund or lucky enough to hit the lottery or (same thing) inherit big bucks from our family, we've got to come up with our own money to invest. And if we don't generate any savings—or generate only a piddling amount—then all the investing savvy in the world isn't likely to

43

help us create enough money for goals like buying a house, sending the kids to college, and funding a secure retirement.

Aside from the obvious notion that you can't invest and earn a return on money you don't have, there's another reason why becoming a diligent saver is crucial for creating wealth. You have a lot more control over how much money you can save than over how much you can earn on investments. Granted, your ability to save is somewhat limited by how much you earn and the living expenses you face. Still, anyone who's at all serious about saving can always find a way to pare back some expenses, to spare themselves the occasional, though no doubt well-deserved, luxury and otherwise find ways to set aside a few bucks. There's absolutely nothing you can do, on the other hand, to boost stock returns in a year when the market is flagging. By and large, most investors' gains in stocks and bonds are dictated by the return of the stock and bond markets overall. Even the majority of seasoned pros can't outrun the market averages over long stretches of time.

Another reason that adding to your investment stash from savings is so important is that the flow of new money takes some of the pressure off you to earn lofty returns to meet your goals. For example, if you stash away $2,000 a year and earn an achievable 10 percent return on that money, you will accumulate a little more than $35,000 over the course of ten years. If you had managed to save, say, only $1,000 a year, you would have had to earn a 22 percent rate of return to accumulate the same thirty-five grand. I can't think of too many investments you can count on to churn out 22 percent annual gains over a decade or longer. In fact, I can't think of one.

WHERE DO YOU FALL ON THE SAVER-INVESTOR SCALE?

To illustrate just how much of an effect your savings habits can have on the amount of wealth you generate to meet your financial goals, I've put together a hypothetical example of four different types of people with varying savings habits and investment expertise and how much money each would have after investing and saving through an entire work life. Specifically, in the four scenarios presented, I take a look at 1) someone who is a pathetic saver but a terrific investor; 2) another who is a decent saver and an average investor; 3) someone who is a great saver and a great investor; and 4) someone who combines diligent saving with terrific investing. The four scenarios share some of the same underlying assumptions: namely, each of these fictional persons starts out at age twenty earning $20,000 a year, gets 4 percent annual raises, and stops working at age sixty-five. The idea is to show how different combinations of saving and investing translate to the amount of money that would be set aside for retirement after a lifetime of investing. For simplicity's sake, I didn't deduct income taxes from the returns in these examples.

PATHETIC SAVER–TERRIFIC INVESTOR: This person manages to save only 1 percent of his salary each year, which means in the first decade of his career he's putting away just a few hundred bucks a year. That savings rate is pitiful, to say the least, since the average savings rate in the United States is more like 4 percent or so of pretax income. Still, as pathetic a saver as this person is, he's doing better than many Americans. A 1995 survey by *Money* magazine conducted by ICR Survey Research Group of Media, Pennsylvania, found that 20 percent of Americans say they're not saving any money at all.

When it comes to investing his puny savings, however, this person does a wonderful job, earning 12 percent annually year in and year out. Unfortunately, superior investment returns alone can't create a significant amount of wealth; you've got to have money on which to earn that return. So after twenty years on his meager-savings-great-investing track, this person has acquired only a little over $15,800, and by age sixty-five his savings total a bit more than $440,000. That's not much money to see anyone through retirement, since the average sixty-five-year-old man who doesn't smoke has about a 40 percent chance of living to age ninety and as much as a 10 percent shot of making it to one hundred.

DECENT SAVER–AVERAGE INVESTOR: Most of us (by "us," I mean people who show enough concern about their money to be reading this book) are probably like this person, who saves 5 percent of her income each year and earns a respectable 8 percent. The 5 percent savings rate is a tad above the 4 percent or so average for most Americans, but remember that the average includes lots of people who save zilch. So it's not farfetched that someone showing the slightest will to save would easily manage to sock away 5 percent or so of her income each year. As for the 8 percent return, that's also easily achievable by investing in a conservative 60/40 percent blend of stock and bond mutual funds. What's amazing is, solely by virtue of her willingness to sock away more of her money on a regular basis, how much more wealth this person accumulates than the pathetic saver with terrific investing skills. After 20 years the decent saver–average investor has more than $53,000, and by the time she's ready to call it a career at age 65, she's got more than $700,000.

GREAT SAVER–GREAT INVESTOR: The great saver–great investor combines a formidable will to save—putting away 10 percent of his salary annually—and also manages to boost his investing returns to an average 10 percent annually. The effect that combination has on the amount of money the great saver–great investor accumulates is nothing less than astounding. After 20 years this person parlays his twin traits of disciplined saving plus superior investing skills into an investing stash worth nearly $130,000. In another 10 years that stash has grown to more than $400,000, and by age 65 this person has acquired about $2.5 million—or more than three times as much as the decent saver–average investor and more than five times as much as the pathetic saver–terrific investor. If the decent saver–average investor category is the one that most of us now fall into, the great saver–great investor category is the one we should aspire to. I think it's achievable for most people, although moving from the second category to this one depends largely on whether you have the will to forgo current spending so you can reach your financial goals and boost your standard of living in the future.

TERRIFIC SAVER–TERRIFIC INVESTOR: This paragon of self-discipline, foresightedness, and investing skill manages to sock away an impressive 12 percent of her income each year and earn an equally impressive 12 percent return on that money. That combo of a high savings rate and superior returns creates a staggering amount of wealth: after twenty years this person would have an investing account with a balance of more than $190,000 and by age sixty-five would be sitting on a pile worth more than $5.3 million, or more than double the amount even the great saver–great investor would have.

Of course, I've got to admit that I don't believe you will run across many such people in real life, and I doubt that many of us can pull ourselves far up enough the savings-and-investing ladder to become this type of person. It's not the investing part that I see as the main obstacle. I think 12 percent returns, though historically high, are at least in the ballpark for someone who puts together an aggressive blend of large- and small-company stock mutual funds and a slight sprinking of bonds—and who is willing to hang on during the occasional steep drops such a portfolio will undoubtedly suffer.

Rather, I see saving 12 percent of income as the main stumbling block for most people, since it requires one to save about three times as much as the average American. Still, I think many people could gradually work themselves up to this group. Early in your career, when you're making less money and budgets are tight, saving 12 percent is probably unrealistic. But if you don't fall into the trap of automatically sopping up your raises with more spending, I think it's possible to move into the 12 percent savings bracket or an even higher one, as your income rises.

The chart shown here traces year by year the amount of money each of our four hypothetical saver-investors accumulated over their work lives. Aside from the fact that I went to a lot of trouble creating multiple computerized spreadsheets for this chart, I have two reasons for putting it here. The first is so you can see just how striking the differences are in the amount of money you can create when you save diligently. In fact, I labeled this section "Where *Will* You Fall on the Investing-Saving Scale?" because I think it's important to see not just where you are now, but where you can be if you put a bit more (but hardly a Herculean) effort into saving and investing. I see the top two lines on the chart as goals we can all shoot for without becoming ascetics who do nothing but deny ourselves pleasure and devote every waking moment to investments.

The second reason I want you to see this chart is that it reinforces a point I made in the first chapter about starting to invest as soon as you can. Notice how all four of the lines on the chart—and especially the top two—really start picking up steam as you move to the right? And in the top two lines in particular, see how steep the lines become? Well, what's driving all the lines upward in those later years, when the hypothetical saver-investors are in their fifties and sixties, isn't the money that's being saved and invested in those years, but the compounded gains of all the money that was invested way back at ages twenty, thirty, and forty.

Let's take the example of the terrific saver–terrific investor.

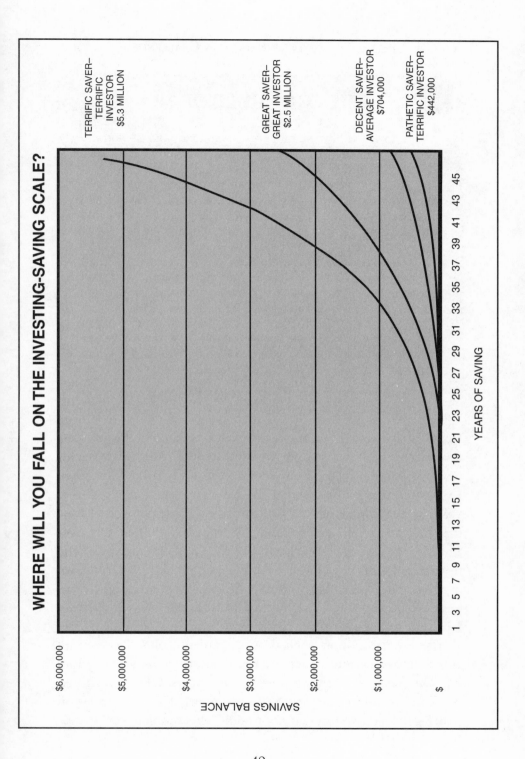

WHERE WILL YOU FALL ON THE INVESTING-SAVING SCALE?

TERRIFIC SAVER–TERRIFIC INVESTOR $5.3 MILLION

GREAT SAVER–GREAT INVESTOR $2.5 MILLION

DECENT SAVER–AVERAGE INVESTOR $704,000

PATHETIC SAVER–TERRIFIC INVESTOR $442,000

SAVINGS BALANCE

$6,000,000
$5,000,000
$4,000,000
$3,000,000
$2,000,000
$1,000,000
$

1 3 5 7 9 11 13 15 17 19 21 23 25 27 29 31 33 35 37 39 41 43 45

YEARS OF SAVING

THE COOL RULE OF 72

Want to know how many years it will take your savings to double at a given annual rate of return? Just take the number 72 and divide it by the annual return you expect to earn. If your savings grow at 8 percent a year, for example, your money will double in nine years (72 divided by 8) and quadruple in eighteen years. (If you want to take taxes into account, take 72 and divide it by your annual after-tax rate of return.)

This rule works in reverse, too, letting you figure out the return you must earn to double your money within a certain period of time. So if you need to double your stash in, say, six years, you know you must earn 12 percent annually.

Remember, though, the Rule of 72 isn't magic. It tells you only what return you *must* earn to double your money; it says nothing about what you actually *will* earn. The market—and to a lesser extent your skill as an investor—determines that.

Between age sixty-four and sixty-five, for example, this person's investment stash has grown by almost $600,000. That's right, nearly $600,000 in the course of a year. Only a bit more than $13,000 of that six hundred grand was the amount added in that year's saving contribution from earnings (12 percent of a salary that had grown 4 percent annually from $20,000 to just over $112,000 by age sixty-four). Most of the $600,000 increase came from the earnings on all the even smaller contributions from savings in earlier years. For example, the $2,400 the terrific saver–terrific investor salted away at age twenty has grown to almost $394,000 alone after forty-five years of earning 12 percent. Add all the other amounts socked away annually, plus the years of compounded earnings over the years, and that's why those lines start skyrocketing straight up in the later years. Of course, if you don't invest any money early on—or you get a late start—you won't get that awesome compounding effect, unless you decide to work and save and invest till you're ninety-five and then leave it all to your ungrateful heirs.

WHY YOU WON'T FIND ONE OF THOSE DUMB SAVINGS WORKSHEETS IN THIS BOOK

About this point, anyone familiar with the personal finance genre of writing as currently practiced in most books and the popular magazines knows that there is usually an obligatory worksheet that purports to tell you exactly how much money you've got to set aside each month or year to meet financial goals like putting the rug rats through college or accumulating a retirement stash. I know you've seen these worksheets before. They typically start by asking you how much of your current income you'll need in retirement (75 percent is usually the figure you're told to shoot for, even though you may need way less or lots more, depending on factors such as your health and whether you've paid off your home mortgage) or the cost of a particular goal, like the $3 trillion or whatever it will take to make your budding genius a member of the Harvard class of 2016.

You're then supposed to estimate things like the inflation rate over the next twenty years (as though you really know what that will be), the tax rate you'll face, and other imponderables. Finally, you go through the worksheet to find that in order to save what you need, you will have to start putting away $3,000 a month for the next forty years. Of course, since your paycheck after taxes is only $3,100 a month, you realize you've got a little problem— like how to explain to your bank that you won't be paying your mortgage anymore because it's interfering with your long-term plan for financial security.

Well, I don't believe those types of worksheets are much help. For one thing, they can scare people away from saving at all. By that I mean that after people complete them they often find that the amount they supposedly need to save is so daunting, they get discouraged and don't even bother to start to save. If you feel that having a specific dollar target helps you, then you should try one of the popular CD-ROM programs, such as Intuit's Quicken, or go to one of the Internet sites, such as *Money* magazine's (www.moneymag.com), that have calculators that let you figure out how much money you must save and invest to meet certain goals. But I think the better approach for building your savings is simply to get into the habit of saving regularly—preferably each month, but quarterly could work, too—and then try to increase your savings as you go along. You can and should occasionally calculate what percentage of your annual income you're setting away—and I think 10 percent or more is a reasonable goal for you to aspire to—but what's most important is becoming comfortable with the discipline of regular saving so that it becomes a natural part of your financial life.

MY SIMPLE BUT EFFECTIVE FOUR-PRONGED SAVINGS STRATEGY

So how do you cultivate the habit of saving consistently without relegating yourself to a lifetime of drab self-denial? Here are my four suggestions:

1. WRITE DOWN WHAT YOU SPEND. Usually, the first thing a financial planner or other financial expert recommends is that you rev up one of the budgeting CD-ROM programs such as Quicken or Microsoft Money, divide all your spending into categories ranging from, say, mortgage payments to utilities to groceries, and then create an official budget for yourself. That's fine, if creating pie charts of your household expenditures on a regular basis is your idea of a rollicking good time. But I've got an easier low-tech route that will also work: just write down every expenditure you make over the course of about a month or so.

Be sure to add in other major expenses that might not have occurred in the month you've chosen for this exercise, such as the cost of your annual vacation or your property taxes if they're not included in your monthly mortgage payment. When you do this, you will quickly see where most of your money is going and where you have opportunities to cut back. You won't be sur-

WHATTA YOU WANT—FAST FOOD OR $100,000?

How many times a week do you grab something at McDonald's or order a Domino's pizza rather than eat leftovers? Once, twice? (Just what *are* leftovers?) And how much do you spend by the time you add in sodas, fries, McDonald's scald-the-roof-of-your-mouth apple pies, or extra cheese and pepperoni from Domino's? Twenty-five bucks a shot? Well, consider this: If just once a week instead of feasting on fast food or pizza you throw $25 into a mutual fund that earns a modest 8 percent annual return, you would have just over $100,000 after twenty-five years. That's right, a hundred large. Okay, maybe that kind of disciplined long-term savings is too high a hurdle for many of us. But even if you managed this feat twice a month, allowing you to sock away $50 monthly, you would still have $17,000 after fifteen years and almost $48,000 after twenty-five years. With a chunk of cash like that, you'll be able to do a lot better than Happy Meals and Pepperoni Pizza Feasts.

prised by big items like mortgage and auto loan payments, but you might be shocked to find out how much "leakage" there is in your budget—lunch, dinner, or drinks with friends that can run into a hundred bucks a month or more, impulse purchases like the $89.95 you shelled out for that boxed set of K.C. and the Sunshine Band's *Greatest Marginal Disco Hits* (with the hour-long version of "Shake Your Booty"). In any case, by putting down on paper every cent you spend and how you spent it, you'll have your spending patterns right in front of you, where you can analyze them.

2. LOOK FOR PLACES TO PARE SPENDING. Once you've got a record of your spending in front of you, you can see where the best opportunities are for cutting back. You should probably start with the biggest expenditures, since they offer the potential for the largest savings gains. No, I'm not suggesting you simply give up making mortgage payments. But you might consider whether you can lower your monthly payment by refinancing your loan.

Then start looking for smaller sacrifices you can make without drastically altering your lifestyle. Is the $100 a month you spend at McDonald's and ordering in from Domino's really a non-negotiable expense? Do you need *every* premium cable TV channel there is, or can you get by with the one you watch the most? Find enough of these small nonessential expenses that you can slim down or eliminate altogether and you may be able to come up with an extra $1,000 or so a year in investable cash just from discretionary items alone.

3. BE REALISTIC. If you try to eliminate all luxuries from your life and go on a crash spending diet, chances are you'll feel deprived, get disillusioned, and whip out the old credit card to make up for lost time. So start your savings programs slowly to get a feel for what works and what doesn't. Make sure to leave some indulgences for yourself, however. After all, you're looking only to cut back spending. You shouldn't be trying to adopt the lifestyle of a Trappist monk, unless spiritual fulfillment is your ultimate goal.

4. REEVALUATE YOUR PROGRAM EVERY FEW YEARS. Once you've begun to save regularly, you should go over your budget occasionally to see how you're doing. For one thing, you might find that despite your best efforts, you have slid back into some of your old expensive habits. (First clue: Your credit card is getting worn from having it swished through that machine so many times.) But even if you've stayed on the straight-and-narrow savings trail, there's another reason to reevaluate your spending habits: There might be new opportunities to save that popped up in the past few years. Maybe after a few years of salary raises, you can afford to salt away even more money than you're already setting aside.

EIGHT SIMPLE WAYS (AND ONE DRASTIC ONE) TO BOOST YOUR SAVINGS AND GENERATE SOME INVESTABLE CASH

Okay, now you're ready for some tips on how to increase your savings. I'm going to assume that you've already done the obvious thing and rooted through every chair and sofa in your house and come up with, oh, a buck and a half or so to get you started. Good job. Now we can really get to work. What follows are nine suggestions that can help you come up with some real cash to invest. (I know all lists are supposed to have ten items, but I could come up with only nine that made sense.) I suggest you think of these as dishes on a smorgasbord. Peruse them, see which appeal to you, sample a few to see how you like them, and settle on those that make the most sense for you.

1. SAVE YOUR RAISE. The next time you get a raise, just imagine it never happened. That's right, just pretend your employer hasn't showered you with the extra moolah and, instead, invest the extra money from your paycheck. You can generate some serious savings by doing this. If you're earning, say, $40,000 a year and your employer rewards you with a 4 per-cent increase, you will have an extra $1,600 a year, or about $133 a month, before taxes, and roughly $1,150, or $95 a month, after federal taxes. If you're not saving already, this is a pretty good start. If you already are setting money aside, this is a good way to turbocharge your savings. You won't be able to do this with every raise you get—that would mean living on the same salary your entire life—but if you can pull off this feat every few years and stick to it, you can effectively boost your savings while also raising your standard of living.

2. REFINANCE YOUR MORTGAGE. Clearly this tip is going to work only if a) you own a house and plan to live in it a while; b) you have a mortgage on it; and c) interest rates have fallen by at least a half percentage point or more since you took out your home loan. But if you meet these three criteria, chances are you can lower your monthly housing expenses by lowering your mortgage payment. For example, let's say your present $150,000 thirty-year fixed-rate mortgage carries an 8.5 percent interest rate, which makes your mortgage payment roughly $1,150 a month. If the going rate on new thirty-year fixed-rate loans has dropped a full percentage point to 7.5 percent, the same $150,000 loan would cost you only $1,050 a month, for a savings of $100 a month. (If you have an adjustable-rate mortgage whose rate has climbed above the current rate for a fixed-rate loan, you should also consider refinancing.) Since the interest portion of that payment is tax-deductible, your after-tax payment and after-tax savings are somewhat lower. But on a cash-flow basis alone, you would still have an extra $100 a month to funnel into investments. Of course, you'll probably have to shell out closing costs when you refinance, so don't even bother with this strategy unless you think you'll be around long enough to recoup those costs in the form of lower monthly payments. If rates have fallen a percentage point or so—and you're paying two to three percentage points of the loan amount in closing costs—it usually takes two and a half to four years for that to happen.

3. FORGO THE FLASHY WHEELS. Nothing beats the thrill of going from zero to sixty mph in three nanoseconds in a flashy ragtop or cruising around town in one of those big-bruiser SUVs that can transform you from Mr. or Mrs. Sedan-Nerd into the Ultimate Road Warrior—but is it worth hocking your financial future for the privilege? By forgoing the pleasure of intimidating other drivers on the highway with the sheer menacing bulk of a 1998 Ford Explorer XLT 4WD and opting instead for an admittedly more wimpish Subaru Legacy wagon, you could save an estimated $5,000 over five years in total ownership costs—that is, the difference in sticker price plus annual operating and maintenance expenses and depreciation. To compare the ownership costs of new cars, check out the Complete Car Cost Guide (IntelliChoice, San Jose, California, 800-227-2665) or visit IntelliChoice's Web site (www.intellichoice.com).

4. FIGHT TO LOWER YOUR PROPERTY TAXES. Depending on where you live, the yearly property taxes you pay can range from a minor annoyance to a significant financial drain. In 1997, for example, property taxes on a typical 2,200-square-foot home averaged more than $3,000 in twenty-five states and totaled more than $6,300 in New Jersey. In some states the tab you pay may also vary widely by county. So, for example, while the average in New York State is just over $6,100, in affluent counties like Westchester, many homeowners pay double that figure.

By challenging your assessment, you stand a good chance of cutting your property tax bill. Roughly half the people who challenge their property assessments win reductions of 10 percent or more. So if you're paying $5,000 annually in taxes and get a 10 percent break, you'll have $500 the first year of the reduction and even higher savings in future years, since property taxes generally tend to go up, not down. For a booklet explaining how to go about challenging your assessment, send $6.95 to the National Taxpayer's Union at 108 N. Alfred Street, Alexandria, Virginia 22314. There are also many companies that will fight to lower your taxes for you—for a fee, of course. You will usually pay one-half to one year's worth of the tax savings that the firm wins for you.

5. PRUNE YOUR PLASTIC. There's no doubt about it—Americans are in love with credit cards. According to RAM Research, a Frederick, Maryland, firm that tracks credit card debt, the typical U.S. household with credit cards had an average total card balance of almost $4,500 going into 1998. Considering that the average rate charged by credit cards runs about 18 percent a year, someone who kept that $4,500 balance steady throughout the year would pay over $800 annually in interest payments. But interest charges aren't the only way that credit cards can bust your budget. There's some evidence that we're willing to pay *more* for something if we're paying with plastic rather than cash. MIT professors Drazen Prelec and Duncan Simester performed an experiment in which half the people who participated in a sealed-bid auction for tickets for a Boston Celtics game were told they would have to pay in cash, while the other half were told they would pay by credit card. So what happened? The people paying by credit card bid twice as much on average as the people who had to use hard cash.

It's impractical today simply to chuck your credit cards, but you can use them less often. Try going "plasticless" for a month to see if your spending declines when you have to shell out cash every time you buy something. And if your credit card carries a rate at or above the 18 percent or so national average, then in addition to scaling back your credit card use, look for a card with a lower rate. You'll find the best deals on credit cards—as well as lots of helpful info about mortgage, home-equity, and car loans—at Bank Rate Monitor's Web site (www.bankrate.com).

6. FIRE UP THE MICROWAVE (AND EAT OUT LESS OFTEN). Americans eat an average of four meals outside the home each week. Of course, dining out is often more a time-saving necessity than a luxury these days. But it can run into some real bucks nonetheless, costing roughly $140 a month for the average U.S. household and probably much more for busy two-income families. Cut down the number of times you dine out to twice a week—after all, you can always nuke a frozen entrée in the microwave and chow down within five minutes—and you can pick up $70 or so a month in investable cash.

7. BE A SAVVY SHOPPER. Here's a quick quiz: By joining discount warehouse clubs like Sam's Club and Price Club, you can a) buy your olives in convenient fifty-five-gallon drum containers; and b) save more than 20 percent compared with what you would pay at other retailers.

Both answers are right, sort of. I have seen some huge jars of olives (as well as frighteningly large containers of mayonnaise) at these discount warehouse joints. As for the savings, all I can tell you is that according to *Money* magazine, the Food Marketing Institute found that on average, these clubs offer 26 percent savings over retail competitors. Again, I wouldn't bet on getting exactly 26 percent. But considering that the average American household spends more than $4,200 a year on groceries alone, even whittling 10 percent from that tab translates to savings of $35 a month. Which isn't bad, as long as you have the space to store those industrial-size jars of spaghetti sauce.

8. SET UP AN AUTOMATIC SAVINGS PLAN. One of the best ways to prevent yourself from spending too much is to save your money before you can actually get your hands on it. For example, if your employer offers a tax-deferred retirement savings plan such as a 401(k), you should definitely consider enrolling. These plans automatically deduct pretax dollars from your paycheck, so they offer not only the discipline of forced savings, but a tax break, too.

Once you've got your 401(k) or other company savings plan rolling, consider trying to put away more money by starting an automatic investing plan. Many major mutual fund families run automatic investing plans, which transfer money from your bank account to your fund account every month. You may have to put up anywhere from $250 to $5,000 or more to get the account started, but after that many fund companies require additional investments of as little as $50 to $100 a month. By buying fund shares automatically each month, you not only invest conveniently and painlessly, you also end up practicing dollar-cost averaging, one of the best strategies for building wealth in the long term.

9. RELOCATE TO CHEAPER DIGS. Granted, the trading-down option is a radical move (literally) and probably isn't worth exploring if you have roots in a particular city or neighborhood or a job that requires you to stay in the area where you now live. But since the cost of living can easily vary 10 percent to 20 percent from one city to another, you can free up some serious money for investing if you do have the flexibility to relocate. You can get a good idea of the possible savings by checking out the ReloSmart relocation software (800-872-2294; $49.95) sold by Right Choice, a Salem, Massachusetts, company that tracks living costs in some eight hundred U.S. cities. For example, when I plugged in my own financial profile, I discovered I could lower my living expenses by more than $10,000 a year by moving, say, from the suburbs of New York City to Atlanta, Georgia.

If picking up and moving is too big a change, you can also probably find less expensive neighborhoods near where you now live. For that matter, if you live in a large house, you could consider trading down to a smaller, less expensive place in the same city. After all, now that real estate values aren't cruising along at a double-digit pace as they were during the 1970s housing boom, it's not as if you're racking up incredible amounts of equity in your home that you can retire on. Besides, the tax law passed in 1997 lets married couples keep profits of up to $500,000 and single owners profits of as much as $250,000 on their principal residence without paying tax on those gains. So most homeowners would get to sell their house without having to relinquish much of their gains to the IRS.

MONEY-MARKET FUNDS: THE IDEAL STASH FOR READY CASH

Now that you're stripping all the fat out of your bloated budget, the question is, where do you put that money? Eventually you'll want to be tucking most of it away in stocks or stock funds and bonds or bond funds.

Before you even *think* of putting money into those investments, however, you should have at least three to six months' worth of living expenses set aside in a money-market fund: that is, a mutual fund that invests almost exclusively in short-term debt securities such as Treasury bills and commercial paper

YOU WANT A MONEY-MARKET FUND, *NOT* A MONEY-MARKET ACCOUNT

Anxious to keep your savings in their vaults, most banks now offer their own version of money-market funds. They're called money-market *accounts.* But unless you're interested in enriching your local banker, I'd say avoid them. The biggest shortcoming in these inferior substitutes for money funds is the way their rates are determined—that is, they're set by the banks, which seem to use Ebenezer Scrooge as their role model. It's not unusual for bank money-market accounts to pay anywhere from one-quarter to a full percentage point less yield than what money-market funds are paying.

True, the bank money-market account is insured by the Federal Deposit Insurance Corporation, which means your money is safe if the bank fails. Money-market funds have no federal insurance. But the risk of losing money in a money fund is minuscule. In my opinion you're much better off in a money fund run by an established mutual fund company than you are in a bank money-market account. A growing number of banks now offer money-market accounts *and* money-market funds. No doubt this is a sign that more and more bank customers are recognizing money-market accounts for the lousy deal they are. So if you have money in a money-market account, move it to a money-market fund—then you can laugh all the way from the bank.

(essentially corporate IOUs). Unlike bond and stock mutual funds, whose net asset values fluctuate up and down with the financial markets, money funds keep their shares priced at $1 apiece. This $1 per share asset value isn't guaranteed, but it's a value the money funds strive to maintain and so far have been successful in doing. In a handful of highly publicized cases in 1994 and 1995, a few money funds came close to letting their value slip below $1 a share, or "breaking the buck," as it's known in money fund land. But from the time money funds were first launched in the early 1970s, only one has ever lost money, about 4 percent of its value after investing in complicated and risky securities known as *derivatives*. Only institutional investors owned that fund, no individuals. In short, therefore, money funds offer a high degree of safety, generally pay better returns than you'll get from a bank savings account, don't charge penalties for early withdrawals as bank CDs do, and give you quick access to your money. (You can write a check or have money wired from the money fund to your checking account.)

All these features make money funds a near perfect place to stash cash for life's little unanticipated setbacks, like being down-sized from a job or having unexpected medical expenses dumped on you. A money fund is also where you should put savings you may need to draw on soon. If you're saving for a house down payment or a car you plan to buy within a few years, for example, a stock or bond fund would be a risky venture. Why? Its value could decline just when you need to tap into it—and you might not have enough time to wait for stock prices to rebound. By keeping dough for short-term goals in a money-market fund, you'll get decent, if unspectacular, returns—but also the security of knowing that every cent you tucked away, plus interest, will be waiting for you when you need it. Of course, if money funds are so safe, you may ask, why not stick all your money in them? Well, you could if you didn't mind earning anemic returns—and seeing your savings actually lose ground to inflation.

A NO-BRAINER WAY TO CHOOSE A MONEY FUND

Fortunately, picking a money fund is a pretty simple affair. Most of them invest in the same types of securities, so there's not much a manager can do to outgain his peers. In fact, about the only reason some money funds' yields are higher than others is that they charge lower annual expenses. (Beware: Some money funds temporarily waive expenses to jack up their yields.) So my checklist for finding a decent money fund is pretty short. Look for the following:

1. A FUND THAT CHARGES RELATIVELY LOW EXPENSES ON A REGULAR BASIS. The fund's expense ratio tells you how much the fund charges to oversee the portfolio on an annual basis. The figure is expressed as a percentage of assets. The average expense ratio for all money-market funds runs about 0.6 percent to 0.7 percent of assets, which means you're paying $.60 to $.70 per $100 invested for the manager to run the fund. Since expenses are deducted directly from the income the fund earns, lower expenses means more money for you. Generally, if you stick with funds that keep their expense ratios below 0.75 percent, you'll do just fine. The fund's telephone rep should be able to tell you what the fund's expense ratio is.

2. A FUND RUN BY A LARGE MUTUAL FUND FIRM. On the off chance that your money fund ever did run into trouble, a large fund company would probably be more ready to step up to buy troubled securities from the fund or do whatever it had to do to make shareholders whole.

3. A FUND THAT'S CONVENIENT FOR YOU. If you already have an account with a brokerage or fund firm, you may want to use that firm's money fund because it's more convenient. Just check to make sure the fund isn't charging outrageously high expenses. If it is, you have to wonder whether the company is nicking you in other places as well.

There are dozens of money funds that would make perfectly acceptable stashes for your money, and by consulting a newspaper or personal finance magazine, you should have no trouble finding them. But if you would like a few names of money funds that have reasonable expenses, offer competitive returns and are managed by well-known fund families, you'll find them in the following table. If you're in the 28 percent or higher tax bracket, you might consider a tax-exempt money fund. If you're a belt-and-suspenders kind of investor, you might consider a money fund that invests only in U.S. government securities. The fund telephone reps should be able to give you details on these other choices, if you're interested.

FIVE MONEY FUNDS WORTH A LOOK

Fund Name	Expense Ratio[1]	Minimum Initial Investment[2]	Telephone (800)
Vanguard MMR—Prime Portfolio	0.32%	$3,000	662-7447
Fidelity Cash Reserves	0.49%	$2,500	544-8888
T. Rowe Price Prime Reserve	0.63%	$2,500	638-5660
American Century–Benham Prime	0.60%	$2,500	345-2021
Schwab Money Market	0.75%	$2,500	435-4000

[1]As of July 1998
[2]Lower minimums typically apply for IRA accounts.

CHAPTER 3

A Quick and Painless Stint in Investing Boot Camp

••••••••••

Now that we've laid a few general ground rules about investing and talked about the importance of being earnest savers, we can take a closer look at your main investment options. As I mentioned earlier, I believe not only that you can get by with just three types of investments, but that you're much better off limiting yourself to those three—namely, stocks (or, more likely, stock mutual funds), which should be your core investment for long-term goals; bonds (or, more likely, bond mutual funds), which deserve an important, though not starring, role in your portfolio; and cash (most likely money-market funds), which plays a bit part.

Since we've already covered money funds in the previous chapter, I'll devote the bulk of this chapter to explaining how the other two types of investments work and what each can do for you. We'll also talk about the "r" word (risk) and the right way to evaluate it, discuss what you should do about big bad bear markets, and finish up with some guidelines on how to decide whether you should invest primarily in funds or individual stocks and bonds.

STOCKS AND STOCK FUNDS: THE STARS OF YOUR INVESTMENT LINEUP . . . AND WHAT THEY HAVE IN COMMON WITH THE ROLLING STONES

Whether you think the Rolling Stones are the greatest rock-and-roll band of all time or a bunch of aging has-beens who don't know when to pull the plug on their guitars, or even if you don't think of the Stones at all, the one thing you've got to admit is that they have staying power. From the time they first burst onto the rock scene in the sixties with "Satisfaction," through the disco-dominated seventies, the punk era of the eighties, and the grunge craze of the nineties, Mick Jagger and the Stones have managed to weather pop music's various fads and trends and retain a spot at the top of the hierarchy of rock bands. True, they haven't been at the peak of the pop charts every year, and the band has definitely had its ups and downs in music and, judging by the deep fault lines etched into guitarist Keith Richards's face, in life. But for more than thirty-five years the Stones have churned out hard-driving rock and roll to several generations of fans.

So what's this have to do with investing in general and stocks in particular? Simple. When it comes to staying power, stocks make the Rolling Stones look like one-hit wonders. And it's this staying power—the ability to give shareholders satisfaction in the form of superior returns over long periods of time—that makes stocks the cornerstone of any long-term investing strategy.

For the past century, a period that has witnessed recessions, a depression, world wars, political scandals, political scandals, and more political scandals, stocks have been the undisputed superstars of the investment world. Like the Stones, stocks haven't topped the charts every year. But over long periods of time stocks have generated better returns than virtually any other investment for investors patient enough to hang in for the long-term payoff.

What kinds of long-term gains are we talking about? Consider this: If you had invested $10,000 in the Standard & Poor's 500 index (see the next page for an explanation of the S&P 500) at the start of 1943, the year Mick Jagger was born, you would have $9.1 million before taxes by the end of 1997, when he and the Stones were launching their *Bridges to Babylon* tour. That represents nearly a 13.2 percent annualized return over fifty-five years. If you had let your money languish in a bank account during that time, by contrast, you would have had less than $1 million.

Now, the value of your ten grand didn't explode straight upward during this period. There were more than a few rocky stretches, in fact, a total of eleven years during this fifty-five-year span when stocks *lost* money. In 1973, for example, stocks fell 14.8 percent and then dropped another 26.4 percent in 1974. Which means the $430,900 your original ten grand would have grown to from 1943 to the end of 1972, when the Stones released their *Exile on Main Street* album, would have shrunk by more than $160,000 by the end of 1974, the year *It's Only Rock 'n' Roll* debuted. So to get the long-term gain for the entire period, you would have had to prove you had the stones, so to speak, to hang on just when it appeared that the market was falling apart.

You've also got to keep in mind that the return over this 1944–1997 span was unusually high because you would have been getting into the market at an especially auspicious time— just after it had been decimated by the 1929 crash and the 1930s depression and just before the huge upswing after World War II.

WILL THE REAL "MARKET" PLEASE STAND UP?

TV anchors tell us whether the market is up or down for the day, advisers counsel us about getting into it or out of it, thousands of putative experts track it and have opinions on it. But what, exactly, do they mean by the market? Here's a look at three market indexes you should know about:

1. The Dow Jones Industrial Average. Although this index has become virtually synonymous with the stock market, it's not a particularly good gauge for stocks overall. Why? Because it contains the stocks of only thirty large U.S. companies that are chosen by a bunch of editors at *The Wall Street Journal* (which is owned by Dow Jones & Co.) and that represent just 20 percent of the stock market's total value. Still, the Dow has longevity going for it—Charles H. Dow first began calculating it in 1896—and it's the one you're most likely to hear cited in daily news reports.

2. The Standard & Poor's 500 index. A much better proxy for the overall stock market than the Dow, the S&P 500 tracks the stocks of five hundred large, widely held U.S. companies. They're not the five hundred largest firms; rather, they're five hundred companies a bunch of people at investment research firm Standard & Poor's consider good representatives of a broad spectrum of industries. The market values of the five hundred firms in the index account for about 70 percent of the market value of all publicly traded U.S. stocks. But the S&P 500 has its downside, too: the largest one hundred companies in the S&P 500 are so big that changes in their stock prices alone can wipe out the impact of the other four hundred stocks. Still, because it represents a good chunk of the market and is easily accessible, this index is probably the best market barometer for most investors.

3. The Wilshire 5000 index. Despite the "5000" in its name, this index actually measures the performance of more than seven thousand publicly traded companies from the largest to the tiniest. Since it tracks the prices of virtually all stocks with readily available price data, the Wilshire 5000 is probably the most accurate gauge of the overall stock market. Although the index is published in *The Wall Street Journal* and other major newspapers, it's not one that registers on most individual, or even many professional, investors' radar screens. You're probably better off just following the more accessible S&P 500.

You would have also gotten the full benefit of the exceptional bull market of the eighties and nineties. So you were sort of getting in near a low point and counting your gains while the market was really rockin' and rollin'. Which is to say, basically, you lucked out. Long-term stock returns aren't typically that high. Still, this example is particularly apt for today, since stock market returns in the eighties and most of the nineties have also been unusually generous, giving many investors the false sense that such lofty returns are the norm rather than the exception.

INVESTING 101: THE DRIVING FORCE BEHIND THE STOCK MARKET'S ROCKIN' RETURNS

When you buy a share of stock, you're essentially buying a piece of a company's profits. And by and large it's a company's earning power, the money a business can generate for its owners after expenses, that determines its value. So it's not surprising that stock prices generally follow the path of corporate profits. Nor is it surprising that the overall trend in both corporate profits and stock prices is generally upward, since companies in a growing economy tend to make more and more money each year. (The businesses that don't make money eventually go broke, unless they're run or subsidized by the government.)

To get an idea of how stock prices and earnings interact, take a look at the chart on page 73. The dotted line represents the earnings per share of companies in the Standard & Poor's 500 from 1982 through the end of 1997. The black line shows the level of U.S. stock prices, specifically the value of the Standard & Poor's 500.

Clearly there's been a distinct upward trend in both corporate profits and stock prices. But notice that the two lines sometimes converge and then widely diverge. That happens because investors are constantly reevaluating how much they're willing to pay for a dollar's worth of corporate earnings. When investors are dubious about stocks' future earnings potential, they're wary of paying a lot for companies' profits. Similarly, investors are also less willing to pay up for corporate profits when interest rates are high (because investors can earn decent returns in safer investments like bank CDs) and when they believe that inflation may be on the rise (because corporate profits may not be able to keep up with inflation).

When the earnings line is above the stock price line in the chart on page 73 (as was the case in early 1982), that indicates investors are a bit skittish about stocks. For the year ending in the first quarter of 1982, for example, the companies in the S&P 500 earned $14.81 per share on average, and the S&P 500 index stood at 112. That means investors were willing to pay almost $8 for each $1 of profits ($112 divided by $14.81). This ratio of stock prices to earnings is known as the *price-earnings ratio,* or *PE,* and it's basically a barometer of how investors feel about the future prospects for the stock market overall. When calculated for an individual stock, the PE represents what investors think about the outlook for that stock. (In reality, investors are paying for their estimate of *future* earnings, but for simplicity's sake—and because projections of future earnings are guesstimates at best—I'll use historical earnings in this example.)

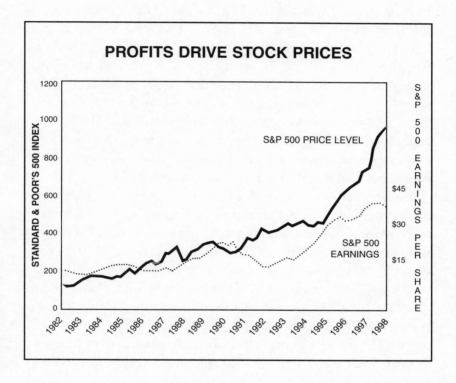

STOCK EUPHORIA CAN TURN TO STOCK MANIA

In August 1982 stock prices began a powerful upward surge as investors began to feel the outlook for the economy was improving and that, at a PE of 8, stocks looked like a screaming bargain. And by late 1987, with the bull market in full swing, investors were positively euphoric. PEs were now hovering above 20, which means investors were willing to pay 2½ times as much for $1 of corporate earnings as they had been in early 1982. Generally, investors have been willing to pay $14 to $15 for each $1 of corporate earnings. Whenever the two lines in the chart actually come together, the market PE ratio was roughly 14.

But look at how far the two lines have grown apart since the beginning of 1995. Yes, the trend is still up in both cases, but the stock market has basically decoupled from earnings. If investors were euphoric about stocks in 1987, then during the 1990s they became stock maniacs, frenetically trading stocks online and pouring billions of dollars into stock mutual funds ($231 billion in 1997 alone). As a result of this all-consuming desire to own stocks, investors bid up stock prices to the point where they were paying $24 for $1 of corporate earnings. Some market prognosticators claim that a PE of 24 is easily justified. The economy in the mid-1990s was strong, the outlook for corporate profits healthy, and interest rates and inflation were low and didn't appear poised to flare up in the future. Pessimists, on the other hand, noted that at a PE of 24, one of the highest ever for U.S. stocks, stock prices left no margin for disappointment, the possibility that the economy and businesses might fall short of our incredibly rosy expectations.

But as the market seers debated this issue, the market continued to soar, churning out an unprecedented string of double-digit returns: 37.5 percent in 1995, 23 percent in 1996, and 33.4 percent in 1997. Over those three years alone, stock investors *more than doubled their money.* And when you combine those years with other healthy returns in the late eighties and early nineties, stock investors on average *quintupled* their money for the ten years to January 1, 1998, enjoying a total gain of 428 percent, or an annual total return of 18.1 percent.

GET REAL ABOUT FUTURE STOCK RETURNS

The question is, of course, are such returns sustainable over the long term? No one knows for sure, but I don't see how the huge returns of the 1980s and 1990s can be duplicated over the next ten or twenty years. I don't know when it will happen or how it will occur. Perhaps the market correction that sent stocks tumbling for losses of roughly 20 percent between July and September of 1998 was the beginning of such a retrenchment process. But one way or another, the stock market will pull back from its incredible charge and returns will fall back to a more normal range.

Okay, I don't actually *know* that stock returns are headed lower in the future. No one knows what the market will do. But I strongly *suspect* it for several reasons. For one thing, whenever there's a stock market mania like the one in recent years, it's usually followed by a big sell-off. A boom-and-bust mentality is probably just part of human nature. We get carried away with something—whether it's tulip bulbs in seventeenth-century Holland, Los Angeles real estate in the early 1980s, or stocks and stock mutual funds in the 1990s—throw our money at it, and convince ourselves that the good times will last forever. Then a bit of bad news surfaces or some independent soul questions why we're paying such outrageous prices for stocks, and suddenly no one can remember why in the world they thought stocks were such a great buy at average PE ratios of 24 or what possessed them to buy Yahoo! stock when it traded at the dizzying PE of 254.

Before you know it, stocks go from the "gotta have 'em" to the "gotta get rid of 'em" stage, and investors can't dump their stocks fast enough. Then all those lines on stock charts that were pointing steeply north have suddenly turned due south, and the rout is on. And typically that's what happened when stock prices got way ahead of earnings in the past. As a result, whenever we've had periods of unusually high returns in other decades, they've been followed by much milder gains. For example, after the market churned out 19 percent annualized gains in the nifty 1950s, investors had to settle for 8 percent gains in the 1960s and even more meager 6 percent annual returns in the 1970s.

 ## YOU CAN'T ALWAYS GET WHAT YOU WANT . . . BUT TIME, TIME, TIME IS ON YOUR SIDE

I doubt Mick Jagger was thinking of the stock market when he sang "You Can't Always Get What You Want." But the line can apply to stocks. Investors who poured money into stocks at the market's high in 1973 definitely didn't get the gains they were seeking; they got hit with big losses when the market plunged 48 percent between January 1973 and October 1974. Similarly, anyone who invested in stocks back in August 1987 saw the value of his stash drop 33 percent over the next few months. Those declines were especially severe, but over the past eight decades the market has dropped 10 percent or more about eighty times.

As the table below shows, however, time is on your side. The longer you stay invested in stocks, the greater your chances are of making money.

THE LONGER YOU INVEST,
THE BETTER OFF YOU ARE IN STOCKS

If you invest in stocks for . . .	The odds of losing money are[1] . . .	The odds of beating bonds are[1] . . .	The odds of beating inflation are . . .	Stocks' best return[2]	Stocks' worst return[2]
1 year	28 %	65 %	68 %	54 %	-43 %
5 years	10 %	85 %	79 %	24 %	-12 %
10 years	3 %	84 %	89 %	20 %	-1 %
15 years	0 %	78 %	93 %	18 %	1 %
20 years	0 %	98 %	100 %	17 %	3 %

Source: Author's calculations based on data from Ibbotson Associates. Used with permission. © 1998 Ibbotson Associates, Inc. All rights reserved. (Certain portions of this work were derived from copyrighted works of Roger G. Ibbotson and Rex Sinquefield.)

[1]Based on calendar-year returns from 1926 through 1997.
[2]Annualized returns.

This doesn't mean I'm predicting dismal returns for the next ten years or suggesting you bail out of stocks. On the contrary, I still believe stocks should remain the core holding for long-term investors. Even if their returns fall off a cliff, I would expect them to outgain bonds over the very long term. I am saying, though, that it would be foolish to count on the 18 percent returns of the past ten years to continue for another decade or, for that matter, even to count on the 13 percent annualized return from 1943 through 1997. So in terms of setting your *expectations* for stock returns over the long term, I think it's more realistic to think in terms of 8 percent to 11 percent a year—about the range for long-term average returns over this century—rather than 13 percent to 18 percent.

Keep in mind, too, that these average returns are just that—averages over long periods. You won't get them unfailingly year after year; there will be setbacks along the way, where stocks can lose 10 percent, 20 percent, or even more of their value temporarily. So getting to those long-term averages will involve not just riding the boom years, but struggling through some bust years as well.

BONDS AND BOND FUNDS: THESE RODNEY DANGERFIELDS OF THE INVESTMENT WORLD STILL DESERVE A PLACE IN YOUR PORTFOLIO

If stocks are superstars of the investing arena, bonds are the nerds that get no respect. That's because, when it comes to generating superior returns, bonds have eaten stocks' dust for most of this century, generally trailing stock returns by five to six percentage points a year. And even though bond returns have been especially generous from the mid-1980s into the late 1990s, they still haven't kept up with the phenomenal returns of stocks. For the ten years through 1997, bonds overall gained a bit over 9 percent a year, while stocks returned nearly twice that, or 18 percent.

It makes perfect sense, of course, that bonds should generally return less than stocks. They are, after all, inherently a less risky investment. When you buy a bond, you are essentially lending money to a company in return for their legally binding promise to pay you interest (at a rate known as the *coupon rate* of the bond) and to repay the original amount you lent (the principal, or face amount, of the bond) at the end of the bond's term. If the company breaks that promise, say, because it runs into financial difficulties, the bondholders have a claim on the company's assets. So even if the company goes bankrupt, there's a good chance you may still get back a portion of your principal, although it may take years of legal wrangling.

Bonds are also less risky than stocks in another way. The prices of bonds tend to be more stable than the prices of stocks, partly because bonds pay regular interest payments that help cushion them somewhat from steep drops. Over long periods of time, bond prices tend to bounce up or down only about one-third to one-half as much as stock prices.

If you're a long-term investor looking for the highest possible returns, why should you bother with bonds at all? One reason is that since bonds don't move exactly in synch with stocks, they often manage to post gains (or sustain smaller losses) in years when stocks lose money. In nine of the ten calendar years from 1953 through 1990 in which stocks had negative returns, bonds stayed in the black. So if you held a combination of stocks and bonds, the bonds would have provided a bit of a cushion in those years, gaining 9.5 percent in 1981 when stocks lost 5 percent, for example, and returning 9.7 percent in 1990 when stocks declined 3.1 percent. I don't want to overstate this cushioning effect. In the severe market downturns of the early 1970s, when stocks lost 14.8 percent and 26.4 percent in 1973 and 1974, respectively, it's not as if bonds' positive returns of 4.6 percent and 5.7 percent would have made you whole if you were invested mostly in stocks. Still, had you held 60 percent of your money in stocks and 40 percent in bonds going into that two-year slump, the value of your portfolio would have declined about 18 percent—a withering loss, to be sure, but a hell of a lot better than the 37 percent decline a stocks-only portfolio would have suffered.

The other reason it's a good idea to devote a portion of your portfolio to bonds is that after trailing stocks so badly in recent years, bonds could possibly overtake stocks in the near future—or at least significantly close the performance gap. A recent study by mutual fund firm T. Rowe Price suggests the chances of that happening are pretty good. T. Rowe Price found six 5-year periods between 1960 and 1990 during which stocks outgained bonds by at least nine percentage points a year. The firm then examined the returns of both stocks and bonds in the five years immediately following each of those six initial five-year spans to see how bonds fared after trailing stocks so badly. T. Rowe Price found that in all but one of the subsequent five-year periods, bonds narrowed the performance gap considerably, often closing it to a few percentage points a year. In one case bonds even out-performed over the following five years.

So will bonds make a big comeback after trailing stocks so badly in recent years? Beats me. All I know (make that "strongly suspect") is that stocks can't keep up their recent pace for another decade. So it's not a bad idea to have some bonds in your mix of investments to hedge your bets. Precisely how much you should have in bonds depends on what kinds of temporary losses you can stomach and how quickly you're going to need the money you've got invested. In chapter 7 we'll go into more detail about determining the right stocks-bonds mix for a variety of situations.

WHY SAFE IS RISKY AND RISKY IS SAFE

When it comes to assessing the risks of investing, most people, to paraphrase the immortal words of *The Catcher in The Rye*'s Holden Caulfield, get it back-asswards. They see the big risk as the chance that stock prices will collapse and they'll be facing big losses. To avoid that danger, they hunker down in what they consider the "safe" course, sticking their money in Treasury bills, money-market funds, or bank accounts.

That foxhole approach makes sense if you're dealing with money you'll definitely need within a few years. But if you're investing for long-term goals that are five or more years away—like retirement or future education costs—that "safe" approach is actually highly risky. You may protect yourself from short-term dips in stock prices, but you leave yourself vulnerable to an even bigger danger—namely, that the purchasing power of the money you put away won't keep pace with inflation.

For example, if in the beginning of 1987 you had put $10,000 into a six-month bank CD and rolled that money over every six months to the beginning of 1998, you would have successfully avoided the October 1987 crash, when stocks lost 22 percent, and the 15 percent dip in stock prices from June to October 1990—and your ten grand would have grown to $19,100, an average annual return of 6.1 percent. But after paying annual income taxes on your CD earnings during that time, your annualized return would have dropped to roughly 4.4 percent, assuming a 28 percent tax rate. What's more, inflation over that time averaged 3.5 percent a year, which means that with respect to what your after-tax dollars could buy, your return was cut to just 0.9 percent annually. So in terms of *after-tax purchasing power,* your $10,000 actually grew to a bit more than $11,000.

Had you invested the same $10,000 in stocks, you would have

seen your stash lose money during the October 1987 crash and the 1990 setback. But over the entire eleven-year stretch, you would have earned a 16.8 percent annual return before taxes and inflation and an estimated 8.6 percent return after taxes and inflation. So in terms of real purchasing power, your ten grand would have grown to roughly $24,800, or $13,800 or so more than with a CD. (Actually you would probably have done even better in stocks. That's because to keep the example simple, I assumed you paid taxes on your stock gains every year at a 28 percent tax rate. In reality you would not pay taxes on appreciation in shares you didn't actually sell during that period. And you would pay only a 20 percent maximum rate on shares you sold but held more than twelve months. So your effective tax rate on stock profits would likely be lower than 28 percent.)

There's no guarantee you'll do as well in the next ten years, of course. But over long periods of time, stock returns have generally beaten inflation by six to nine percentage points annually, while short-term investments like CDs are lucky to outrun inflation by one percentage point a year. The longer your investing time frame, therefore, the *less* risk you actually take by investing in stocks and the *more* risk you take by buying "safe" investments like bank CDs. So even though it might sound like Big Brother double-speak, the fact is that when it comes to investing for long-term goals such as retirement, safe is risky, and risky is safe.

HOW TO SURVIVE
A BIG BAD BEAR MARKET

Of course, it's easy to talk about the virtues of staying the course with stocks when they deliver double-digit gains. But people's perspectives—and their stomach for risk—often change when a bear market lumbers in. A bear market is generally defined as a 20 percent-or-better decline in a stock index like the Dow Jones Industrial Average or Standard & Poor's 500 index. When stock prices drop by at least 10 percent but less than 20 percent, market analysts usually use the euphemistic term *correction,* as if stock prices were somehow wrong beforehand and needed to be set right.

Although the market's periodic downturns can seem devastating when they occur, you would be making a big mistake if you pull out of stocks during such a downturn or, for that matter, if you let the prospect of a prolonged market decline scare you from investing in stocks at all. Similarly, I think it's a big mistake to let the threat of a bear market lead you to change your long-term investing strategy. When stock prices reach what many analysts agree to be precariously high levels, some investment advisers, investment publications, and other putative market seers often begin advising investors to cut back their stock holdings and to shift their money into bonds or cash equivalents like money-market funds or Treasury bills.

The problem with that advice: While you're funneling your money into supposedly defensive investments with lower returns, the stock market could go right on generating superior returns for days, weeks, months, even years. Fact is, no one can predict exactly when a bear market will kick in, so I think it's useless and ultimately self-defeating to try to rejigger your investments on the chance stock prices will decline. Instead you should set a mix of stocks, bonds, and cash that makes sense given your investing time frame (as described in chapter 7), and stick with that mix whatever the market is doing.

Still, it doesn't hurt to have a game plan in mind for when a bear market does hit, so you won't get rattled. Here's my three-point plan for surviving a bear market:

1. STAY CALM. Market setbacks are a fact of life. In this century stock prices have dropped by at least 5 percent more than twice a year on average, by 10 percent about once a year, 15 percent every three years, and 20 percent once every five years. And although there's really nothing you can do to change the course of a bear market or a smaller slide in prices, you can at least take solace in knowing that eventually it will give way to another bull market.

How long that will take is anybody's guess, but in the past it's taken investors two to four years to recoup bear market losses. In truly grizzly bear markets, it can take even longer. In the 1973–1974 bear market, stock investors were in the hole nearly ten years. Fortunately not all bear markets are that severe, so it's not as if you should plan for the value of your stock holdings to remain underwater for a decade. On the other hand, if you're going to need your money within three or so years, then it *shouldn't be in stocks in the first place*—even if the market's returns look attractive.

2. DON'T SELL. The worst mistake you can make during a market downturn is to bail out of stocks, figuring you'll get back in when the market looks healthy. The problem with that strategy (if you want to call it a strategy) is that you have no way of knowing when it's time to get back into the market. Stocks often have explosive gains in the early stages of a new bull market. Miss out on those early gains, and you won't get the full benefits of stocks' long-term superior returns.

3. KEEP INVESTING. I'm always amazed that people are willing to pour immense amounts of money into stocks or stock funds when prices are rising. But if the market takes a 20 percent dive, suddenly they want nothing to do with stocks or funds. Hey, if you thought these were worthwhile investments at $100, aren't they an even better deal at $80? If you are choosing fundamentally sound companies whose stocks are selling at reasonable prices—or your fund manager is doing that for you—then the fact that stock prices have fallen shouldn't change your long-term outlook. If anything, it should make you more optimistic about the money you're investing during the setback, since you're getting the same companies for less money.

Although you can never know for sure which investing strategy will come out ahead in the future, the evidence suggests you would do best during a bear market by continuing to invest regularly in stocks. Investment firm T. Rowe Price looked at how three different types of investors, each with $10,000 invested in stocks going into each of the six bear markets of the past thirty years, would have fared by following three different strategies: the *confirmed stock investor* not only stayed in stocks, but invested an additional $100 each month in stocks; the *cash investor* sold stocks once the market had declined 10 percent and then put the proceeds, plus an additional $100 a month, in Treasury bills; the *switcher* duplicated the cash investor's moves, except he then moved his entire account back to stocks after the market returned to its pre–bear market level. What T. Rowe Price found was that in the relatively short bear markets of the 1980s and 1990s, the confirmed stock investor caught up to the cash investor and the switcher relatively quickly. For example, after suffering through a 33 percent decline that lasted from late August till early December 1987, the value of the stock investor's account had surpassed the cash investor's and switcher's by July 1989, less than two years from the market's pre-crash peak.

The bear markets of the late 1960s and early 1970s were generally longer and occurred during periods of high inflation, so it took the confirmed stock investor a longer time to catch his cash and switcher counterparts. For example, it wasn't until 7½ years after the start of the 1973–1974 bear market—during which stock prices declined 48 percent—that the confirmed stock investor finally pulled ahead.

Clearly 7½ years is a long time to keep the faith. But fortunately bear markets like the one in 1973–1974 have tended to be pretty rare (so far, at least). Besides, this example looks only at the stock holdings of the confirmed stock investor. If the confirmed stock investor had also stashed a portion of his portfolio in bonds—as recommended in chapter 7—then the loss in his overall portfolio wouldn't have been as severe as the stocks–only portion, and the overall portfolio would have recovered its value more quickly than his stock holdings alone.

TEN SIGNS THAT THE STOCK MARKET MAY BE TOO HIGH

No one can foretell market slumps in advance with any degree of accuracy. But by checking out several key market indicators, you can at least get a sense of when stock prices are trading at unrealistically high levels.

Following are ten signs that can help you determine if the stock market may be climbing to unsustainable levels. The first five are based on data that reflect the underlying value of stocks or investors' sentiments about the market. The second five are real–life signs that things on Wall Street are just getting too crazy and that stock prices are vulnerable to a setback. Remember, though, the mere fact that stocks seem overvalued isn't a reason to sell. Stocks can and do trade at high levels for a long time, and bailing out early can mean missing substantial gains.

FIVE INVESTING INDICATORS THAT
STOCKS MAY BE OVERPRICED

1. PRICE-EARNINGS RATIOS ARE BLIMPISH. As more people clamor to put their money in stocks, investors bid up stock prices, driving up PE ratios. It's not uncommon to see the market's PE double or even triple during a bull run. If stocks fall short of the lofty expectations those PE ratios represent, however, investors may dump their stocks and push down stock prices. Since PEs vary substantially depending on the level of interest rates and the outlook for inflation and corporate profits, there's no fixed standard for what constitutes "too high." But any time the PE ratio exceeds 18, you can probably figure stocks are headed toward overvalued territory, if not already there, and if the PE exceeds 20, the stock market may be breaking into the realm of "irrational exuberance."

2. PRICE-TO-BOOK RATIOS ARE BLOATED. The price-to-book value ratio shows what investors are willing to shell out for $1 worth of the assets a company owns. To calculate price-to-book ratios, statisticians divide the company's share price by the company's net assets per share, which equals the value of all the company's assets minus all liabilities. If a company's shares trade at $20 apiece, and the company has $20 in total assets and $10 in total liabilities, then the company has net assets of $10 and the stock has a price-to-book ratio of 2 ($20 divided by $10 of net assets). As with the PEs, it's hard to say exactly when the market's overall price-to-book ratio is unrealistically high. Historically, though, price-to-book for major market indexes has averaged about 2.5. So once you get much above that figure, and certainly once you get into the ratios of 5 to 1 and higher that prevailed in 1998, it's pretty clear that stock prices are approaching wishful-thinking land.

3. THE MARKET'S DIVIDEND YIELD IS TOO SLIM.

The dividend yield—the annual dividend a company pays divided by its current stock price—is another gauge of whether investors are bidding up stock prices to insane levels. To calculate the dividend yield for the market as a whole, analysts take the dividends paid by companies in an index like the Dow Jones Industrial Average or S&P 500 and then divide that figure by the stock prices of the companies in the index. As stock prices rise quickly, the dividend yield drops. Value-conscious investors begin to get concerned that stock prices may be too high when the dividend yield for indexes like the Dow and S&P fall below 2.5 percent or so.

4. THE MARKET HAS BAD BREADTH.

No, we're not talking halitosis here. Rather, market breadth is an indication of whether the market's advance is broadly based, or being led by a smaller number of widely held shares. The main way technicians measure breadth is by calculating an advance/decline line, which is basically a running tally of the difference between the number of stock issues rising or falling each day. When gainers outnumber losers, the line goes up; when losers dominate, the line falls. Even if the market overall is still rising, a downward-trending advance/decline line means that fewer and fewer stocks are pushing the market upward—and more and more stocks are tugging downward. If that trend continues, the losers should eventually overpower the winners, knocking the stock market overall downward.

5. INVESTORS ARE TOO BULLISH.

The outlook for the stock market is rosiest when the overwhelming majority of investors are euphoric, right? Wrong. For stock prices to advance, money must flow continuously into stocks. Normally that money would come from pessimists who had previously been hesitant about investing. But when virtually everyone is a bull, there are not enough bears left to nudge the market upward. And since the rush of former-bears-converted-to-bulls into the market has probably bid up share prices beyond their reasonable values, it's likely that any bad news could send stock prices tumbling.

There are a number of so-called sentiment indicators technicians consult to determine whether investors are getting too giddy. A common one is looking at the percentage of investment advisers who are bearish. Generally, when the number of bearish advisers slips below 20 percent, it is considered negative for the stock market. Another indication that investors may be crossing the line from investing to speculating is when they begin snapping up shares of small, untested companies in initial public offerings by obscure brokerage firms in the hopes of scoring huge profits quickly. Whatever the measure, the general rule is that the more investors love the market's prospects, the more you should be wary of a possible downturn.

FIVE REAL-LIFE SIGNS THAT THE MARKET IS OVERPRICED

If you don't want to spend your free time poring over market statistics, there is another way of gauging whether stock prices are getting frothy. Just look around you. Here are five real-life indicators that stock-market bulls might be pushing stock prices to unsustainable levels:

1. WALL STREET PROS ARE SPENDING THEIR MONEY ESPECIALLY LAVISHLY. As a bull market climbs to a crescendo, investment advisers, brokers, and other Wall Street pros begin raking in huge, almost obscene, amounts of money. With all that money sloshing around, some of it inevitably finds its way into what I can only describe as dubious projects. For example, one investment adviser devoted an entire page of his monthly newsletter to a detailed account of his latest home-improvement project—installing a heated driveway that would automatically melt ice and snow. It was an undertaking that involved installing underground heating elements that would kick in at different times and regrading portions of the driveway so that the melted runoff from one area wouldn't refreeze on another section. As I read his account, I couldn't help but think back to the excesses that preceded the 1987 crash.

2. MORE SHOPS POP UP THAT CATER TO FRIVO-LOUS NEEDS. President Reagan's trickle-down theory was roundly criticized in the 1980s. But in cities where the brokerage industry has a strong presence, there is such an effect when the Wall Street money machine is whirring along at high speed. Retailers and other merchants catch the unmistakable scent of huge amounts of discretionary dollars being spent and open up ventures that would never fly on Main Street, USA. In New York City, for example, a company called the Art of Shaving operates two stores on Manhattan's East Side where customers can enjoy a "royal" shave for $45—or buy their own shaving accoutrements, including a $280 silver-tipped badger brush or a horn-handle razor with deluxe stainless-steel blade for $280. By the way, the Art of Shaving's second store was opened just two months before the Dow plunged 554 points on October 27, 1997. Coincidence?

3. HOUSE PRICES GET BID UP TO RIDICULOUS LEVELS. The Wall Street crowd that inflates stock prices by plowing billions of dollars into a relative handful of well-known stocks exercises pretty much the same herd mentality when deciding where to buy their homes. So when you see 2,500-square-foot four-bedroom Colonials with no apparent charm in towns like Greenwich, Connecticut, and Bedford, New York, fetching anywhere from $500,000 to $1.5 million—or roughly two to five times what they would cost in less desirable sub-urbs—you've got to wonder if a market top isn't too far off.

4. WALL STREETERS "PARTY DOWN" FOR CHRIST-MAS.

Annual Christmas or holiday parties are an institution on Wall Street—and the higher the stock market climbs, the more lavish the bash is likely to be. In December 1996, for example, in the wake of a 60 percent rise in stock prices over the previous twenty-four months, a *New York Times* article described several Wall Street Christmas parties, including one that featured $190 bottles of Cristal Champagne and another five hundred-person soiree for which flowers alone cost $40,000. When investment firms feel flush enough to spend upward of $400 per person for self-congratulatory Christmas celebrations, you know that a Scrooge of a market correction could be lurking somewhere.

5. POWER SUSPENDERS MAKE A COMEBACK.

During the roaring bull market of the 1980s, the height of sartorial splendor for investment bankers and stockbroker-wanna-be-investment bankers were zany suspenders. (Extra-wide numbers in fire-engine red or decorated with bulls wrestling bears were popular.) Aside from the obvious ostentation of twenty- and thirty-year-olds wearing suspenders (and the added pretension of calling them "braces"), this fashion trend represented an astounding arrogance: Wall Street pros obviously felt they could dress like clowns and people would still give them their money to invest. Of course, the 1987 crash snapped the suspender craze. But Wall Street has a notoriously short memory. When the market climbs to ridiculous heights in the future, investment bankers and brokers might go into their closets and emerge with their power suspenders again. If they do, take it as a sure sign that irrational optimism is outrunning good sense on Wall Street, and brace yourself for a market setback.

INDIVIDUAL STOCKS AND BONDS VS. MUTUAL FUNDS

One final issue before we get to evaluating specific investments—and that issue is, should you be investing primarily in individual stocks or bonds or sticking to mutual funds? I qualify that question with "primarily" because many investors own both. When the Investment Company Institute—the trade organization that's the chief cheerleader for mutual fund companies—polled fund investors in 1995, roughly half of fund owners said they also owned individual stocks. The poll didn't ask how they happened to own these stocks, but I suspect that many of them own shares of their employer that they acquired through a 401(k) plan, perhaps as a matching contribution, or that they received through an employee stock ownership plan or option grant. I doubt that half of fund shareholders are serious stock investors.

Clearly, where you come down on the individual stocks and bonds versus funds issue is largely a personal decision based on how much time you want to spend on your investments, what level of control you want to exercise, how much you like dealing with things financial, and how much you can delude yourself into thinking that you can do a better job of picking stocks than professional fund managers. . . . Oops, my bias is showing, so I might as well come out and admit it: I believe that funds are far and away the best choice for the vast majority of investors. It's possible to do just fine in individual stocks or bonds, of course, but I don't think most people have the time and patience to research, select, and then monitor individual securities. Even more important, I think it's too easy for stock investors to slip into Wall Street's trading mentality. Everywhere investors turn today, they get the message that the more closely you follow the market and the more quickly you act, the more money you make. Acting, of course, means buying or selling securities, which drives up trading commissions and transaction costs and, in my opinion, ultimately builds more wealth for the brokerage industry than for you.

But if you feel you have the time, talent, and inclination for researching and picking stocks—*and you have the discipline to trade only when you feel it's absolutely necessary, not because trading gives you an adrenaline rush*—then you might want to consider investing in individual stocks. If you do decide to take the stocks route, however, I suggest you do it (initially, at least) with a small portion of your portfolio. That way, if it turns out you're not actually a budding Peter Lynch or Warren Buffett, you've put only a little bit of your money at risk. And assuming you haven't blown your entire wad on your terrific insights, uncanny hunches, and bold speculations, you'll be able to win back some of your losses by investing in some decent mutual funds, as explained in the next chapter.

CHAPTER 4

All You Probably Need
Are Mutual Funds

• • • • • • • • • • •

Funds Are Fine . . . It's Fund Companies
That Need Improving

At the risk of sounding like a shill for the mutual fund industry, more than fifteen years of researching and writing about all kinds of investments has convinced me that mutual funds are the way to go for the overwhelming majority of investors, neophytes and veterans alike. That's especially the case if you want your investing activities to remain a not too bothersome sideline rather than the focal point of your life.

Apparently a lot of investors agree. Since 1980 the percentage of American households that own funds has multiplied nearly seven times to just over 37 percent at the beginning of 1998, while the amount of money invested in stock and bond funds soared more than *sixty times* to just over $3 billion.

Why do I see funds as the investment of choice for most investors? Let me rattle off a few reasons:

1. FUNDS CAN MAKE INVESTING RELATIVELY SIMPLE. When you buy shares in a stock or bond fund, you automatically get a piece of a diversified portfolio, usually upward of one hundred or so securities. That diversification doesn't insulate your investment from broad market declines, but it does protect your account's value from being obliterated because one or two stocks fall apart.

2. YOU DON'T NEED BIG BUCKS TO GET IN THE GAME. You can usually get into most funds for a relatively small amount of money (typically no more than $3,000 and sometimes as little as $50 or less). And once you're a shareholder, you can usually make additional investments of as little as $50 or $100.

3. YOU HAVE ACCESS TO PROFESSIONAL MONEY MANAGERS. Many mutual funds are run by the same professionals who oversee money for wealthy individuals, corporations, and large pension funds. If you tried to hire such managers on your own, they wouldn't even talk to you unless you had $1 million or more to invest. But by pooling money from thousands of people like you, funds have access to the best investing talent in the world (although that doesn't assure market-beating returns, as you'll see later in this chapter).

4. YOU CAN CHOOSE FROM A BROAD ARRAY OF INVESTMENT TYPES AND STYLES. Name almost any type of investment—growth stocks, value stocks, technology stocks, foreign stocks, government bonds, corporate bonds, municipal bonds—and you can find a fund that will give it to you.

5. YOU CAN BUY FUNDS ALMOST ANYWHERE. A slight exaggeration, perhaps, but funds are available from a wide range of sources. Cheapskate that I am, I recommend sticking with no-load funds—that is, ones without sales commissions—

that are sold directly by the fund company. But you can also buy from a broker, financial planner, bank, or one of the fund supermarkets. Emporiums such as Charles Schwab's OneSource (800-266-5623) and discount brokerage firm Jack White & Co.'s fund network (800-233-3411) give you access to dozens of fund families' funds, many free of sales charges and other transaction fees. If you plan to hold several funds from different fund families, buying through one of these networks can be convenient and cut the paperwork to a minimum by allowing you to keep all your holdings in one statement.

A FEW NITPICKS ABOUT FUNDS

Of course, there are also some shortfalls to funds you should be aware of. One big drawback: You have a lot less control over when you'll take gains—and pay taxes—with a fund. By law, fund managers are required to pass along to shareholders virtually all income and any gains on the profits resulting from the sale of securities in the portfolio. Nothing wrong with gains, except you have to pay taxes on them. If you own stocks or bonds directly, *you* decide when to take profits and which year to face the tax consequences.

Most of funds' shortcomings, however, have less to do with mutual funds themselves than with the attitudes and business practices of the fund companies that launch funds. At the risk of sounding like an antifund crank, here's a quick rundown of some of the problems with funds:

1. THERE ARE TOO DAMN MANY OF THEM. One of the things that made funds popular to begin with is that they made investing less complicated. Instead of having to sort through thousands of stocks, you could pick a fund and let the manager do the sorting. But now thousands of funds are vying for your attention—more than nine thousand stock and bond funds as of the summer of 1998, which is nearly four times as many as in 1990. It would be great if this growth meant more terrific funds for you to choose from, but for the most part it's just resulted in more funds. In any case, the sheer number of funds out there, all seemingly claiming to be number one over some period of time, makes it increasingly difficult and more time-consuming to pick funds.

2. A FOCUS ON MARKETING LEADS TO SOME INANE FUNDS.

When you look at some of the lame premises behind funds that have been launched in recent years, you can't help but wonder whether the idea came from the investing division or the guys in marketing. Does the Pauzé Tombstone Fund, which invests in undertakers, coffin makers, and cemetery operators, really represent a viable investment strategy, a way for investors to get in below the ground floor on the healthy death industry—or is it just an attempt to stand out in an overcrowded fund field? And how about the Motorsports Associated Growth & Income Fund, which invests mostly in stocks with some connection to auto racing—a fast track to speedy gains or a ridiculously narrow premise that's headed for a wall? These are real funds, folks, I don't make this stuff up. Admittedly these are extreme examples. But over the years fund companies have launched many funds with more marketing glitter than investing substance that ended up costing investors dearly.

3. FUNDS COST MORE THAN THEY SHOULD.

Investors tend to focus on funds' returns, not their cost. Knowing that, many fund companies feel free to charge whatever they can get away with—which is their prerogative, I suppose, since they're businesses, not charities. Still, many funds could easily charge a lot less and still make plenty of money. In fact, a number of fund companies do charge well below the average for similar funds—and you'll improve your chances of success by sticking to such companies.

FUND ECONOMICS 101: FEES AND EXPENSES

Here's a look at the different types of expenses and fees you may run into as a fund investor:

Front-end load: This is the sales charge some funds—appropriately called *load funds*—levy at the time you buy shares of the fund. It typically ranges from 2 percent to 5.75 percent of the amount you plan to invest. This fee is usually split between the fund company and the broker or planner who sold you the fund. If you're choosing your own funds, you're almost always better off in no-load funds (ones that don't charge sales commissions), although there may be rare occasions when a load fund is so good that it's worth the price of admission.

Back-end load: Instead of docking you at the time you invest, some funds charge the fee when you redeem shares. Back-end loads usually start at 5 percent of the lower of the original price or current market value of the shares you redeem during the first year, then drop to 4 percent the next year, 3 percent the following year, and so on until the charge disappears. Some brokers try to pass off back-end-load funds as no-loads. Don't believe it. To pay brokers who sell back-end loads, fund companies tack on annual fees such as the 12b-1 charges (described next) that siphon off 0.25 percent to 1 percent of your account value a year.

12b-1 fee: Sometimes called a *hidden load,* this fee, which can range from 0.25 percent to 1 percent, is basically a marketing charge. Somehow fund companies convinced the Securities and Exchange Commission in 1980 that charging investors a fee to pay for the marketing expenses of luring new investors into the fund would lower expenses in the long run by increasing assets and creating economies of scale. So far, all that's happened is that fund companies have collected billions in 12b-1 fees. You can avoid 12 b-1 fees—or at least onerous ones of more than 0.25 percent—by sticking to no-load funds.

The expense ratio: All funds—load and no-load alike—pass on to shareholders the annual expenses of running the fund. These ongoing operating expenses include the *management fee* for investing the fund's assets and *administrative charges* for record keeping and other mundane chores. These annual fees—including the 12b-1 charge, if any—are totaled together in a figure called the *expense ratio,* which expresses the expenses as a percentage of the fund's assets. The average expense ratio for U.S. stock funds is roughly 1.5 percent (a charge of $15 for every $1,000 you have in the fund), while the typical bond expense ratio is 1 percent ($10 per $1,000 invested).

4. THEIR PROSPECTUSES ARE JUST TOO DAMN BORING. For years financial journalists, including yours truly, have solemnly told investors to read the prospectus cover to cover. After all, the fund prospectus is the legal document that tells you, among other important things, how the fund operates, what fees it charges, and what risks it takes. But the truth is that prospectuses are so boring, they make a three A.M. C-SPAN debate on technical amendments to a tax bill seem exhilarating.

At the encouragement of the Securities and Exchange Commission (SEC), many fund companies have spent the last few years trying to translate the sleep-inducing liability-dodging legalese of the standard prospectus into something approaching standard English. The SEC has also allowed fund companies to experiment with a "profile prospectus," a shorter, simpler version of the regular prospectus. Despite scattered improvement, few prospectuses today pass the Sominex test. So while I still believe you should read this document before investing in a fund—particularly the fee table and the sections dealing with the fund's strategies and risks—I also admit that I'm effectively sentencing you (depending on your reading speed and tolerance for digesting financial babble) to up to two hours of excruciating, mind-numbing boredom.

So how can you reap the advantages funds have to offer while minimizing the disadvantages? The short answer: Focus on what *your* game plan should be—putting together a group of funds that will deliver long-term competitive returns—and filter out everything else. Your goal isn't to sample every new type of fund that fund sponsors' marketing departments spew out. To earn decent returns in funds, you don't have to be a fund savant who can rattle off the top-performing funds of the nineties along with the names of their managers. In fact, I believe the surest route to success in funds is by putting most, if not all, of your money into a type of fund that in some ways is the antithesis of the fund industry—index funds.

THE FUND INDUSTRY'S DIRTY LITTLE SECRET, OR, WHY YOU'RE BETTER OFF IN INDEX FUNDS

With the best business schools in the country churning out a steady supply of expensively educated MBAs who go to work for fund companies, you would figure that mutual funds would have no trouble generating higher returns than those generated by standard market benchmarks like the Standard & Poor's 500 index. After all, fund shareholders are paying managers big bucks to find the best stocks; it's not as though these guys are doing it in their spare time.

But the fact is, the majority of mutual funds don't beat the market in most years. Nor do most beat it over long stretches, although this isn't news most fund companies are eager to share with investors. Take a look at the chart on page 103. In the twenty-two calendar years from 1976 through 1997, there were only eight times that the majority of U.S. diversified stock funds had higher returns than the S&P 500. In recent years the record for actively managed funds has been particularly bad. For the ten-year period ending June 30, 1998, only 13 percent of U.S. diversified funds beat the S&P 500.

There are several reasons so many funds fall short of the market, but for the most part the explanation boils down to basic arithmetic. Combine the returns earned by mutual funds, corporations, wealthy individuals, and pension funds, and essentially you have the average market return. Clearly not all the managers can be above average. So roughly 50 percent will have returns above the average, while the other 50 percent will fall below the average. But you've also got to factor in the investing costs that funds incur—the cost of research, administration, overhead, salaries, and so on. After you deduct these costs from the gross returns of fund managers, the percentage who beat the market *after expenses* shrinks to less than 50 percent. Over periods of ten years or more, typically only 30 percent of domestic stock managers beat the S&P 500 index. So why not just invest with those 30 percent, you say? Great idea. Problem is, no one knows in advance which managers will be the index beaters. Even after outrunning the index for several years, some managers eventually fall behind, and their place is taken by others who may outrun it for several more. In other words, the fact that a manager has beaten the index in the past is no guarantee he or she will continue to do so in the future.

Admittedly there are some complications to the indexing argument. In the case of comparing U.S. diversified funds to the S&P 500, for example, it's true that many diversified funds hold stocks that are smaller than the S&P 500. And that largely

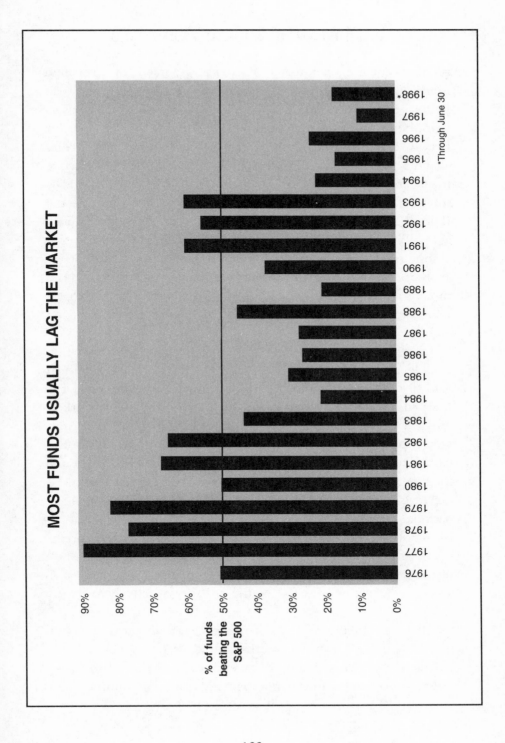

MOST FUNDS USUALLY LAG THE MARKET

% of funds beating the S&P 500

*Through June 30

accounts for the years that more than 50 percent of diversified funds outgained the S&P 500. In those years smaller stocks had higher returns than large stocks. What's more, indexing seems to work better in some areas than others. The case is most solid for large U.S. stocks and bonds, largely because so many securities analysts cover those areas so intensely that it's difficult for active managers to gain an edge on the market. Managers of small-stock funds have historically fared better against their index—the Russell 2000 index of small stocks—than large-company managers. That may be because managers can find better bargains among small stocks that aren't followed as closely by Wall Street analysts. Or it could be because, as their funds attract more money, many small-stock managers begin buying larger stocks, which have done better than small stocks through most of the eighties and nineties.

In recent years international managers have also had little trouble posting higher returns than the standard international yardstick, Morgan Stanley's EAFE (Europe, Australasia, and Far East) index. That's at least partly because Japan's stock market, which represents a large portion of the EAFE index, has stunk worse than rotten sushi the past few years. But in periods in the past, international managers have lagged the EAFE index for long periods, so it would be premature to say that the more recent experience invalidates the concept of indexing for international investors.

If nothing else, indexing assures one thing: that you pretty much get the average market return for whatever stock market or sector you're trying to track. And more often than not, that average return is enough to beat the majority of actively managed funds.

All in all, therefore, I think the case for investors to focus mostly, if not exclusively, on index funds is pretty compelling. They're easy to pick, you don't have to worry about the manager leaving (most index funds are essentially run by computers), and you're assured of earning market-level returns. Of course, if investors moved to index funds in droves, fund companies would be pretty unhappy because the industry's real moneymakers, actively managed funds, would shrink in size, as would the management fees fund companies collect. Boo hoo.

Dozens of index funds are available today, ranging from ones for large-company and small-company stocks to foreign shares to index funds that look for the fastest-growing or most undervalued shares. If you decide to build your portfolio along the guidelines I outline in chapter 7, then you'll probably want to invest in an index fund that invests primarily in large-company stocks such as those in the S&P 500, one that tracks a small-stock index such as the Russell 2000, and, possibly, an index fund that buys international stocks.

Whichever type you decide on, look for one with low expenses. The lower the expenses, the more closely your returns will track the index. In reality, most investors interested in indexing wind up investing with Vanguard because it offers more index funds than any other fund family and because its expenses are downright miserly. The annual expense ratio for its most popular index fund—the Vanguard Index 500—is just 0.19 percent a year, or less than one-seventh of the expenses of the average U.S. stock fund. A growing number of fund families now offer index funds, and I've included a variety of choices in the following table.

IF YOU BELIEVE IN INDEXING, ONE OR MORE OF THESE FUNDS MAY SUIT YOU

Large-Company Funds	Index It Tracks	Expense Ratio	Telephone (800)
Dreyfus S&P 500 Index	S&P 500 index	0.57%	554-4611
Fidelity Spartan Market Index[1]	S&P 500 index	0.19%	554-4611
Schwab S&P 500 fund	S&P 500 index	0.35%	435-4000
Schwab 1000	1,000 U.S. stocks with the largest stock market values	0.47%	435-4000
USAA S&P 500	S&P 500 index	0.18%	382-8722
Vanguard Index 500	S&P 500 index	0.19%	662-7447
Vanguard Index Growth	S&P 500 stocks whose prices are relatively high compared with the value of their underlying assets	0.20%	662-7447
Vanguard Index Value	S&P 500 stocks whose prices are relatively low compared with the value of their underlying assets	0.20%	662-7447
Vanguard Total Stock Market Portfolio	Wilshire 5000 index, which represents the broad sweep of the stock market, from the largest to the tiniest stocks	0.20%	662-7447
Small-Company Funds			
Schwab Small Cap Index	The next 1,000 largest companies after the Schwab 1000	0.59%	435-4000
Vanguard Small-Cap Stock[2]	Russell 2000 index of small stocks	0.25%	662-7447

ALL YOU PROBABLY NEED ARE MUTUAL FUNDS

Large-Company Funds	Index It Tracks	Expense Ratio	Telephone (800)
Vanguard Small-Cap Growth Index[3]	Stocks in the S&P 600 index of small stocks whose prices are relatively high compared with the value of their underlying assets	0.25%	662-7447
Vanguard Small-Cap Value Index[3]	Stocks in the S&P 600 index of small stocks whose prices are relatively low compared with the value of their underlying assets	0.25%	662-7447
International Funds			
Schwab International	The 350 largest foreign stocks	0.58%	435-4000
Vanguard International Equity European[2]	Morgan Stanley Capital International index of European stocks	0.31%	662-7447
Vanguard International Equity Pacific[2]	Morgan Stanley Capital International index of Pacific stocks from six Asian countries, including Japan	0.35%	662-7447
Vanguard International Equity Emerging Markets[4]	An index of stocks from 18 developing nations	0.57%	662-7447
Vanguard Total International Portfolio[2]	Fund buys shares of Vanguard's Europe, Pacific, and emerging markets funds in proportions needed to track foreign stock markets overall	0.35%	662-7447
Bond Funds			
Vanguard Bond Index— Intermediate-Term	Lehman Bros. index of intermediate-term corporate and government bonds; generally has average maturity of about 7 years and duration of roughly 5 years	0.20%	662-7447

Large-Company Funds	Index It Tracks	Expense Ratio	Telephone (800)
Vanguard Bond Index—Long-Term	Lehman Bros. index of long-term corporate and government bonds; generally has average maturity of 22 years and duration of 10 years	0.20%	662-7447
Vanguard Bond Index—Short-Term	Lehman Bros. index of short-term corporate and government bonds; generally has average maturity of just under 3 years and duration of just over 2 years	0.20%	662-7447
Vanguard Total Bond Market	Lehman Bros. aggregate bond index—basically the entire high-quality corporate and government bond market; generally has average maturity of just under 9 years and duration of just over 4 years	0.20%	662-7447

1. Minimum initial investment is $10,000. 2. Fund charges 0.5 percent fee to purchase fund shares to cover transaction costs of buying stocks. 3. Fund charges 1 percent fee to purchase fund shares to cover transaction costs of buying stocks. 4. Fund charges 1 percent fee to purchase funds shares and 1 percent fee to redeem shares to cover transaction costs of buying and selling stocks.

Vanguard charges a $10 annual maintenance fee on all index accounts with balances under $10,000.

IF INDEXING IS SO GREAT, WHY BOTHER WITH OTHER STOCK FUNDS?

If you built a portfolio solely with index funds, I think you would probably do better than the majority of investors. But there is something inside investors that makes them rebel at the thought of sticking only to index funds. Indexing makes intellectual sense, but it's not as much fun as trying to pick a fund that will soar to the top of the performance charts and give you bragging rights at the water cooler. Although I believe it's pretty much impossible to predict which funds will be tomorrow's winners, the impulse to seek out top-performing funds won't lead you to ruin—if you keep it in check.

So I see nothing wrong with a strategy of holding a core of index funds and then filling in around that core with some actively managed funds whose managers have shown they excel at a particular type of investing and maybe have a shot at beating the index or producing comparable returns with less risk. Here is a rundown on the basic choices you have for actively managed stocks funds:

1. VALUE FUNDS: I plead guilty to a bias in favor of value funds—that is, ones that look for stocks that are cheap on the basis of their earnings power (which means they often have low price-earnings ratios) or the value of their underlying assets (which means they often have relatively low price-to-book ratios). I can rationalize my bias by noting that several studies show that over long periods of time, like twenty years, undervalued stocks tend to outperform growth stocks. I would also point out that because undervalued stocks have by definition already been rejected by investors, they tend to get hit less than the market overall when stock prices crumble. But if I strip that away, I've got to admit that what really appeals to me about value investing is that—unlike growth investing, where you're paying top dollar for a stock investors are clamoring for—you're getting stocks at a discount. It's like having an uncle in the stock business.

Large-company value managers typically look for big battered behemoths (call them "black-and-blue chips") whose shares are selling at inexpensive prices. Often these managers have to hang on a long time before their picks pan out; until the rest of the investing crowd catches on to what a good deal an undervalued stock is, the stock price usually remains stagnant. Oakmark fund manager Robert Sanborn, for example, will patiently hold some of his stocks for four years or more.

Small-company value managers typically bottom-fish for shares of small companies (usually ones with market values of less than $1 billion) that have been shunned or beaten down by other investors. For example, Robert Perkins, who manages the Berger Small Cap Value Fund, often buys stocks that he believes have promise but are selling at their fifty-two-week low—that is, the lowest price they've hit over the past year. Another successful small-cap value guy, Royce Premier's Chuck Royce, likes companies that have extremely low debt and dependable growth and are selling below his estimate of their breakup value—that is, the price the company would fetch if it were broken down into smaller pieces that were sold separately.

If you're going to invest in actively managed funds, I believe a value fund is the best place to start. And if you've already got an S&P 500 index fund (or another index fund that contains large companies) in your portfolio, then I think your first value fund should be a small-capper, since it will provide immediate diversification in your portfolio.

2. GROWTH FUNDS: As their name implies, these are funds that invest in shares of companies whose profits are growing rapidly, typically by 15 percent a year or more. The share prices of these funds tend to rise quickly during bull markets but can be hammered for substantial losses—often 20 percent or more—when the market sours. As with value funds, growth fund managers generally focus on either large or small companies. Two good examples of **large-company growth** funds that have produced impressive returns over the years are Dreyfus Appreciation, whose manager, Fayez Sarofim, invests in large, fast-growing household-name companies like Coca-Cola and Merck; and Harbor Capital Appreciation, run by Sig Segalas, who during the summer of 1998 favored large financial stocks such as Citicorp as well as the big drug company Pfizer.

Small-company growth managers, on the other hand, hunt for shares of smaller, often obscure, companies. If you look through the portfolio of a small-growth manager, chances are you would know relatively few of the company names. For example, Edward Jamieson and his team at the Franklin Small Cap Growth 1 Fund—a fund that's racked up a solid record (though it does charge a 4.5 percent load)—have invested in such high-profile firms as UCAR International, a company that makes graphite and carbon electrodes, and Komag, a manufacturer of thin-film disks and recording heads for disk drives.

Theoretically, at least, small-growth funds should generate higher long-term returns than their large-growth counterparts because small companies can generally grow their profits more quickly than behemoths. But what happens in reality is that small-company funds take the lead for a while, often several years, as was the case back in 1991, 1992, and 1993, only to give up the lead to large-company funds in other years. Large-company funds were on top from 1994 through 1997. (That same seesaw effect applies to growth funds versus value-oriented funds.)

If you plan to make an S&P 500 index fund the core of your portfolio, my feeling is you have a better chance at adding diversity and a shot at higher long-term gains by adding a small-company growth fund rather than a large-company growth fund. You can also add a large-company growth fund if you want to emphasize growth in your portfolio, but the chances of overlap in holdings between a large-company growth fund and an S&P 500 index fund are pretty high.

3. INTERNATIONAL FUNDS: Here's where I think you can make a good case for opting for an actively managed fund over an index. For one thing, the index that would make most sense as the benchmark for a broadly diversified foreign stock fund—Morgan Stanley's EAFE index—is heavily weighted in Japanese stocks, because Japan's stock market is so large compared with other foreign equity markets. Investing in any index fund modeled on this benchmark, therefore, is more like making a bet on Japan than simply sampling a broad range of international markets.

So if broad exposure to foreign stock markets is what you're looking for—and that's the reason to put an international fund in your portfolio, as I explain in chapter 7—you can do that pretty effectively by buying a diversified stock fund. You'll have no trouble finding such a fund. Virtually every major fund complex—Fidelity, T. Rowe Price, Vanguard, and American Century-Twentieth Century, to name a few—offers one or more such funds. (One caveat: Don't confuse an international or foreign stock fund with a global stock fund. Managers of global funds have the leeway to put significant portions of their money—often more than half the fund's assets—into U.S. as well as foreign stocks.)

Many major fund groups also offer foreign **emerging markets** funds. These are portfolios that buy stocks in up-and-coming countries, ranging from Latin American markets like Brazil and Argentina to Asian countries such as Malaysia, Thailand, and Korea. In the early 1990s these funds were churning out 25 percent or better annual returns and were considered required investing by many investment advisers. Then the Asian economic crisis materialized in the fall of 1997, and it turned out the miracle economies of places like Malaysia, Thailand, and Korea were papier-mâché.

Result: These funds became submerging markets in 1997 and 1998, and their future looked uncertain at best. So is it worth taking a flier on one of these funds in the hopes of catching it on the rebound? If you're a patient investor with a touch of the gambler in your personality, and you're willing to hang in at least ten years, and you're prepared to weather declines of 30 percent or more in the value of your investment, then, hey, go for it. But I wouldn't invest money I couldn't afford to lose.

4. SPECIALTY FUNDS: There is a slew of different funds that invest in a particular corner of the market: utility funds, technology funds, real estate investment trust funds, precious metals funds, health care funds, and natural resource funds, to name just the ones that immediately come to mind. And some companies slice the salami even thinner than these already narrow sectors: not content to offer just the Fidelity Select-Technology Fund, for example, Fidelity also offers Select-Computers, Select-Electronics, Select-Software/Computers, and Select-Biotechnology. (Hey, c'mon, Fidelity, couldn't you break down that Select-Computers into Select-Monitor, Select-Hard Drive, Select-Keyboard, and Select-Mouse funds?)

My take on specialty funds is that you don't need them to be a successful investor—and buying more than one or two is likely to benefit the fund company more than you. But if you feel like going to the time and trouble to add them to your portfolio, there are instances in which they can make sense, in moderation. A small holding in a fund that invests in real estate investment trusts (REITs) could give you a bit more protection against inflation. What's more, the returns on REIT funds don't closely track those of stocks overall, so REIT funds can make your portfolio less bouncy. And since technology is clearly one of the fastest-growing sectors of the economy, a small position in a tech fund could help boost your returns. And for most investors interested in tech, I think a tech mutual fund is a wiser choice than buying individual tech stocks.

A FEW GUIDELINES FOR CHOOSING STOCK FUNDS

There's no foolproof system for picking superior funds. There's not even a good-enough-for-government-work system. The main stumbling block is that the one thing we know for certain about funds—past performance—isn't very helpful in predicting future returns. Still, by following the guidlines offered here, you at least have a shot at identifying stock funds that can provide competitive returns at a level of risk you can live with:

1. OPT FOR LOW EXPENSES. A fund with lofty gains last year might not post big returns this year. But a fund that had big fat expenses last year will likely charge those hefty fees year after year after year. Since those expenses directly reduce your return, you'll increase your odds of success by avoiding funds with bloated expense ratios. Clearly, with more than 4,800 stock funds around these days, there are going to be some funds that manage to succeed despite high expenses. In general, though, it's hard for high-expense funds to beat their low-cost counterparts over time, as the bar chart here shows.

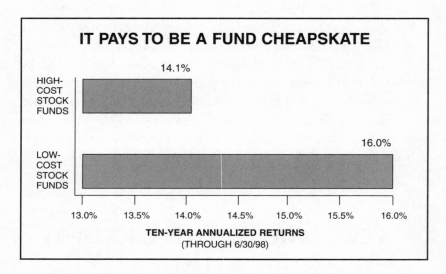

IT PAYS TO BE A FUND CHEAPSKATE

HIGH-COST STOCK FUNDS — 14.1%

LOW-COST STOCK FUNDS — 16.0%

13.0% 13.5% 14.0% 14.5% 15.0% 15.5% 16.0%

TEN-YEAR ANNUALIZED RETURNS
(THROUGH 6/30/98)

2. LOOK FOR CONSISTENCY. For a fund to fit into a diversified portfolio, it's important that the manager stick to a particular investing style. If you bought a fund because you want your portfolio to include, say, small, undervalued stocks, then you don't want the manager jumping into large-growth stocks. The Morningstar report described in chapter 9 can tell you whether a manager has hewed mostly to one style of investing or has jumped around.

3. CHECK OUT THE FUND'S RISK LEVEL. Returns may vary, but funds that are risky, tend to stay risky. So be sure to check out the route the fund took to rack up its past gains and decide whether you would be comfortable with such a ride. (For more on how to gauge the riskiness of a fund, see the box below.)

4. CHECK OUT PAST PERFORMANCE RELATIVE TO PEERS. Why bother doing that, you may ask, if past performance isn't a harbinger of the future? For one thing, you might get some clues about how the fund is managed. For example, if the fund is supposed to invest in small-company growth shares, but its gains are terrific when other small-cap growth managers are hurting, you might have a manager poaching large-caps to juice his returns.

Generally I like a fund to have at least three, and preferably five or more, years of peformance so I can get an idea of how it's done versus funds in the same Morningstar category. And I wouldn't just look at the most recent three or five years' worth of returns. I would examine a variety of periods—single years, down markets, other three- and five-year periods, if possible—to get an idea of how consistently it's performed. For a fund to rate a buy, I would like to see it land in the top half of its peers over most of the periods.

Of course, no past record insures future success. But if I combine this look at past returns with the other three steps I've outlined, I at least know I'm investing in a fund that's done well compared with its peers in past market conditions, has a consistent strategy, has a level of volatility I can handle, and is reasonably priced. That's pretty damn good in a world where there are no guarantees.

RISKY BUSINESS

In the investing arena, risk is usually measured by an estimate of an investment's volatility—that is, how much its value bounces around—or how much its value can sink during a lousy market. Here's a quick look at four risk measures:

Worst quarter: The easiest way to get a quick idea of how much risk you're taking on with a particular fund is to check out its worst quarterly return. You can usually get this figure—as well as the others explained here—from a fund representative or by checking out a Morningstar report.

Beta: This risk barometer measures how much a stock's or stock fund's value jumps around in relation to changes in the value of the S&P 500, which by definition has a beta of 1. A stock or stock fund that's 20 percent more volatile than the S&P 500 would have a beta of 1.2; a stock or stock fund 20 percent less volatile than the S&P 500 would have a beta of 0.8. So *theoretically,* at least, if the S&P rose 10 percent, then a stock fund with a beta of 1.2 would go up 12 percent. The same fund would drop 12 percent if the S&P 500 lost 10 percent.

Standard deviation: This gauge—used more with funds and stock indexes than with individual stocks—tells you how much a stock or bond fund's returns will fluctuate from its average returns. A fund that has a standard deviation of 10 means that most of the time its annualized monthly returns would fall in a range of ten percentage points above or below its monthly average. The higher the standard deviation, the more volatile the fund.

Duration and average maturity: Duration measures how much a bond or bond fund's value will rise or fall in response to interest rate changes. This figure is too difficult and boring for all but hard-core numbers junkies to calculate. But once you know it, you have a pretty high degree of mathematical certainty how your bond fund will react to interest rate changes. A bond or bond fund with a duration of 5, for example, would lose 5 percent of its value if interest rates rise one percentage point. A bond fund with a duration of 8 would lose 8 percent of its value if rates rose one percentage point. The funds would gain the same percentage amounts if interest rates fell one percentage point.

If you can't get a bond fund's duration, you can use the average maturity—the number of years before the bonds in the portfolio must be repaid on average—as a rough proxy of volatility. Average maturity isn't as precise as duration, but generally the longer a fund's average maturity, the more volatile the fund.

WHY INDEXING MAKES EVEN MORE SENSE WITH BONDS

With rare exceptions, indexing generally makes even more sense with bond funds than with stock funds. That's because bond fund managers are all pretty much mining the same vein of bonds—government bonds, corporate issues, and tax-exempt muni bonds—which makes it devilishly difficult for one bond manager to outshine another for an extended period on the basis of investing skill.

Essentially there are only two ways for one bond manager to outperform another. The first is by guessing correctly about the future direction of interest rates. If a manager believes interest rates are headed down, then he or she can load up on long-term bonds, those with maturities of, say, twenty to thirty years. That would boost the fund's returns, because bond prices move in the opposite direction of interest rates, and the longer a bond's maturity—that is, the length of time till its principal must be repaid—the more its price seesaws up or down. On the other hand, if a manager thinks interest rates are headed up, he or she would bulk up on short-term bonds—say, those with maturities of three to five years. (For a fascinating explanation of why bond prices behave this way, see chapter 5.)

A bond manager's gig seems pretty easy, then, right? Just buy long bonds if rates will head up and short bonds if they'll head down. But there's one problem: No one can accurately predict the future direction of interest rates.

The second way bond managers can outperform each other is by going to lower-quality bonds, which carry higher rates than high-quality bonds. That's because the lower the quality of a bond, the greater the chance the issuer might miss interest and principal payments. So by going down even a few small steps on the quality ladder—say, from Treasury bonds to investment-grade corporates—a manager can pick up a bit of extra yield. The more a fund manager dabbles in lower-quality issues, however, the more risk the fund faces. So while piling on risk is certainly an option, it's also cheating in a way, kind of like entering a motor-cycle disguised as a bike in the Tour de France.

EXCEPTIONS TO THE INDEX FUND RULE

There are two instances when you may want to opt for an actively managed bond fund. And the reason in both cases is simply that index funds aren't available for these types of bonds:

MUNICIPAL BOND FUNDS. Municipal funds buy bonds issued by state and local governments. These bonds pay lower yields than Treasury and corporate bonds, but their interest is free from federal taxes. If you buy bonds issued by your state, then the interest is also exempt from state taxes. There are also bonds issued by municipalities and other local government agencies that pay interest that is exempt from federal, state, and local taxes. Double- and triple-exempt bonds can make sense if you live in a tax hell state like New York, California, or Massachusetts.

How do you know whether you're better off in taxable or tax-exempt bond funds? If you own bond funds in a tax-advantaged account such as a 401(k) or IRA, the answer is simple: Avoid muni bond funds. Interest from munis already escapes taxes, so there's no advantage to putting munis in a 401(k) or IRA. You're better off using tax-advantaged accounts to shield the higher yields of taxable bonds from the tax collectors. If you're investing in taxable accounts, on the other hand, then it's a matter of whether the taxable bond pays higher interest than the muni even after deducting taxes. Generally speaking, you shouldn't consider munis unless you're in the 28 percent or higher tax bracket. But to be sure which option is better for you, you've got to compare the taxable and tax-exempt yields on an equal basis. One way to do this: Calculate an after-tax yield for the taxable fund and compare it to the muni's yield. You can do this by subtracting your federal tax rate (say, 28 percent) from 100 percent and multiplying the result (72 percent) by the taxable bond fund's yield (say, 6 percent). If the resulting figure (4.3 percent) is lower than the muni bond fund's yield, you're probably better off in the muni fund. If not, go with the taxable fund. (To compare a double- or triple-tax-exempt fund, you'll have to factor in state and local taxes as well.)

JUNK BOND FUNDS. These funds, which fund sponsors prefer to call *high-yield funds,* buy non–investment grade bonds. Often these are bonds issued as part of a corporate takeover or restructuring or by new companies that haven't established a credit history. Junk bonds have a higher potential for default than government and high-quality corporate bond funds. But since junk funds typically own more than one hundred issues, the high rates of interest these bonds pay (plus the occasional price increases that occur when a junk fund's rating is upgraded) are usually enough to cover losses from a few bad bonds—with enough left over to outperform most other types of bonds over long periods (although junk funds can and do underperform over shorter periods). I wouldn't put a huge portion of my bond holdings into junk. But I don't think you're being wild and crazy if you decide to keep, say, 20 percent or so of your bond stash in these funds.

A FEW TIPS FOR CHOOSING BOND FUNDS

Whether you're buying an index or actively managed bond fund, a taxable or tax-exempt, keep these three guidelines in mind:

1. THINK LOW EXPENSES. The single most important thing you can do to earn competitive returns in a bond fund is to opt for funds with low expenses. That's what makes the bond index funds listed in the table on pages 107–108 so appealing. The minuscule 0.20 percent annual expense ratios of those funds give them a huge advantage over actively managed funds that often charge 1 percent or more a year. It's like running a marathon in eighty-degree temperatures in gym shorts instead of wool sweats. You won't find expenses quite that low in muni bond or junk bond funds, since actively managed funds almost always have higher expense ratios than index funds. Still, when choosing muni or junk funds, stick to funds with expenses that are below average compared with those of their peers. Among the fund companies that keep expenses in the moderate to low range are Vanguard, T. Rowe Price, USAA, and American Century-Benham.

2. STICK WITH SHORT TO INTERMEDIATE MATU-RITIES. Over the past twenty years or so, long-term bond funds have provided the highest returns. No surprise there; they typically have the highest yields, and in the eighties and nineties the overall decline in interest rates meant big price increases for long-term bonds.

But it's not a given that long-term bonds will outperform short-term ones—in the 1970s, for example, intermediate-term bonds regularly beat long-term bonds. What's more, long-term funds can also be surprisingly volatile. If interest rates rise just one percentage point—hey, a frown on the Fed chairman's face can cause that kind of jump—a long-term bond fund can drop

10 percent or more of its value, wiping out more than a year's interest.

If you are a long-term investor *and* you don't mind occasional setbacks like that, long-term funds might be for you. But if you're investing for shorter periods—ten years or less—or if you're using bond funds to add some ballast to a predominantly stock portfolio, then you're better off sticking to bond funds with short- to intermediate-term maturities—say, five to ten years. By staying with maturities within this range, you can typically get 75 percent to 80 percent of the return of long-term funds, while incurring roughly 40 percent or more less volatility than long-term issues.

3. BEWARE TEMPTING YIELDS. Fund companies know that many bond investors home in on yields. So some fund companies do everything they can short of putting the fund on steroids to pump up yields. They may throw some low-grade bonds into a government portfolio, or extend the fund's maturity by buying long-term bonds, or even throw in foreign bonds issued in countries where rates are especially high. These ploys to boost interest may or may not pay off, but they all involve risks that are difficult for shareholders to evaluate. If you see a bond fund that's touting much higher yields than funds with similar maturities and the fund doesn't also have ultra-low expenses, you can be pretty sure the fund is cooking the books one way or another. Don't take the bait; just move on to another fund.

WHEN TO DUMP A FUND

Occasionally in investing, as in marriages or other relationships, things don't work out as planned and you've got to part ways with a fund. Remember, though, a sale could trigger taxes on past gains you've earned. And once you unload a fund, you'll have to find another one, which raises the specter of choosing another dud. So you shouldn't take this step lightly. In fact, the only good reasons I can come up with for selling a fund are these four:

1. YOUR FUND IS A PERSISTENT LOSER. If you own a fund that trails similar funds for two years or more by a substantial margin—say, two percentage points or more a year—and no turnaround is in sight, then I'd unload it. One caveat: The mere fact that a fund has low returns or even posts a loss isn't necessarily a reason to sell. If the overall market is down, for example, chances are your fund will be, too. You can't expect a manager to be a miracle worker and make money when stock prices are plummeting. Similarly, if the types of stocks your manager invests in are out of favor, then your fund's returns may look lackluster even when the broad market's doing fine. So when you're evaluating the performance of a fund, make sure you compare its performance against that of similar funds.

2. THE FUND'S INVESTMENT STRATEGY HAS CHANGED. If you create a diversified portfolio of funds along the lines I suggest in chapter 7, then you're counting on the manager of each fund to invest in a specific way. The small-stock manager should be sticking to small companies, and the value manager should be buying undervalued stocks. But if the small-cap manager has to buy large-company stocks because so much money has been pouring into his fund, or if the value manager tries to pump up returns by throwing in growth shares, then your mix gets all mixed up—and you lose at least some of the benefits of diversification.

3. *YOU* HAVE CHANGED. Yes, sometimes people do outgrow funds. For example, maybe when you were a novice you bought one of those "life cycle" funds that spread their holdings among a variety of different asset classes, including stocks, bonds, and cash equivalents. But after gaining some experience, you decided to build your own portfolio of stock, bond, and money-market funds. If that's the case, then the life cycle fund is probably no longer a good fit, since you have no way of assuring that its mix of assets will jibe with the mix of your overall holdings.

4. A NEW MANAGER CAN'T CUT IT. In today's fund business, many managers job-hop as often as NBA coaches. Any time your fund gets a new skipper, you should monitor the fund's performance to assure two things: first, that the manager is following the same investing style and strategy as his predecessor; second, that performance hasn't suffered. If the strategy does change or performance heads south, I would give the new manager at least one year but no more than two to whip performance back into shape. If that didn't happen, I'd be shopping around for a replacement fund.

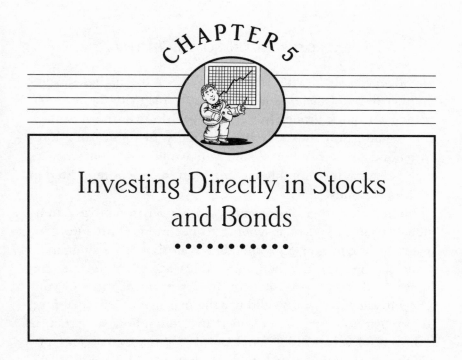

Investing Directly in Stocks and Bonds

••••••••••••

T his may seem like a strange way to start a chapter about investing in stocks and bonds, but in the spirit of full disclosure, here goes: If you never buy an individual stock or bond in your entire life, I don't think you'll be doing yourself a disservice as an investor.

You get a different impression, of course, from many personal finance magazines and cable TV business shows. The implicit message: Mutual funds are the equivalent of investor training wheels. *Real* investors buy individual stocks and bonds.

Well, call me a wimp, but judging by the fact that the majority of professional stock investors don't manage to beat market benchmarks like the Standard & Poor's 500 stock index over long periods of time, I think you're probably better off in index funds that can match a market benchmark.

You can make a stronger case for buying individual bonds,

125

provided you stick with Treasury bonds or the highest-quality municipal bonds *and* hold them until maturity rather than trading for quick profits. But even if you do that, the advantage you would gain compared with sticking your money in a low-cost bond fund isn't huge—and you would lose conveniences such as having the monthly income from the bonds reinvested in additional bonds.

Nonetheless, there are some valid reasons for buying individual securities, if you're willing to put more effort into your investing. Maybe you enjoy spending your time researching individual companies and believe you have a talent for picking stocks. In that case you can save the 1 percent or more of your account value that you would pay the manager of a mutual fund to do that job for you. Or perhaps you follow a particular industry closely, which makes you think you can spot tomorrow's Microsofts or Intels before they're discovered by the Wall Street herd. Buying individual securities clearly has a tax advantage: you decide when to sell, not the fund manager, which gives you much more flexibility for taking taxable gains or, for that matter, taking losses in some stocks that can be offset against gains in others.

In the course of one chapter I can't turn anyone into a stock-picking savant or a bond guru. But if you're interested in trying your hand at individual securities, I can give you a framework for evaluating stocks and bonds, alert you to the risks, and suggest a few ways for you to increase your odds of success. Beyond that, it's up to you to do the research and stay focused on your investing goals rather than getting swept up in the investing horse race.

A DOWN-AND-DIRTY COURSE IN EVALUATING STOCKS

Over the years, an endless succession of Wall Street securities analysts have come up with hundreds, if not thousands, of different methods for picking stocks. But if you boil down these theories to their most basic elements—and throw out strategies based on astrology or its near cousin, technical analysis, a pseudoscience that tracks stocks' price histories and sales volumes—you're pretty much left with two plausible strategies for choosing stocks: growth and value.

GOING FOR GROWTH

As their name implies, growth stocks are shares in companies whose profits have been growing at a torrid pace and are projected to continue their rapid rate of growth into the future. It's the most intuitive form of investing. You buy a company, its earnings grow, its stock price rises. And, all other things being equal, a growth stock's share price should grow roughly in line with its earnings.

Sometimes, astute (or lucky) investors see the share price soar much more than the rate of profit growth via a phenomenon investment pros call *multiple expansion,* a fancy name for a boost in a stock's price-earnings ratio (PE). Let's say, for example, that a company with a history of earnings growth of 15 percent a year earned $3 a share for the past year and now sells for $45, giving it a PE of 15. If the company boosts earnings by another 15 percent next year, it would earn $3.45 and, assuming the same PE, sell for $51.75 ($3.45 times the PE ratio of 15).

But if investors became convinced that over the long term the company could grow at a 20 percent annual pace instead of 15 percent, they might be willing to pay a higher price for future earnings—say, $20 for each $1 of earnings instead of $15. This would boost the stock's PE ratio from 15 to 20. If that happened, the company's stock price on the same $3.45 of earnings would climb to $69, a 53 percent increase from $45 versus the 15 percent increase had the PE remained the same. And if, in addition to commanding a higher PE ratio, the company also increased its $3 profit by 20 percent instead of 15 percent, the stock's price would soar to $72 ($3.60 times 20), a 60 percent increase from $45.

This combination of rising earnings and rising PE ratios is the equivalent of nirvana for growth investors. Of course, the process can work in reverse, too—known as *multiple contraction*. If investors decide a growth stock isn't worth its lofty PE, the stock can get whacked for a big loss. PEs can contract because investors lose faith in a company's earnings power, because the stock market overall is suffering, or because investors fear a spike in inflation, which dilutes the attractiveness of future earnings.

You'll usually find the most opportunities for growth stocks by sifting through the ranks of small companies—that is, ones with revenues or stock market values of $500 million or less. That's not because the executives of small businesses are inherently smarter than the suits in charge of large firms. It's just that as a company gets bigger, it becomes harder for profits to expand at the same fast pace. Still, many large companies manage to churn out impressive earnings gains year after year by churning out new products or finding new markets for existing ones. Coca-Cola's earnings per share, for example, zoomed along at more than 18 percent a year for the ten years to 1998, in large part because the company expanded beyond Coke-sated U.S. consumers to overseas markets.

While the growth companies that get most of the attention today are high-flying technology stocks—the Dell Computers, the Microsofts, the Intels, and virtually any company with .com appended to its name—growth stocks actually span a variety of industries, even distinctly low-tech ones. Take Gillette. How much more basic can you get than a company that sells razors that cut whiskers off men's faces? Not exactly rocket science. But by packaging its razors with fancy names like the Sensor Excel and launching "innovations" like the new triple-bladed Mach 3, the company is able to convince growing numbers of men to pay premium prices for what amounts to sharpened shards of steel embedded in a plastic handle.

What to Look For in Growth Stocks

Rapidly growing earnings and revenues: There's no Growth Stock Commission that issues edicts on exactly how fast earnings must advance for a stock to fall into the growth category. But most growth-oriented investors like to see profits that are chugging along at least 1½ times as fast as those of stocks overall. So, for example, if analysts are projecting that profits for companies in the Standard & Poor's 500 will increase by 10 percent over the next year, you would expect a growth stock's earnings to grow by 15 percent or more.

You also want to make sure profit growth is being spurred by revenue increases, not just cost-cutting. Slashing costs may be fine as a short-term way to boost profits, but you can cut costs only so much. To generate sustainable profit growth, a company must also have growing sales or revenues.

A healthy return on equity: Return on equity, or ROE, is a basic measure of how profitable a company is. This figure is calculated by taking the company's annual earnings and dividing it by its net worth (assets minus liabilities). Ultimately ROE also determines how quickly a business can grow in the future. If a company's not earning a decent return on its capital, its long-term prospects are dim. Generally, growth stocks should have an ROE of at least 15 percent, preferably higher.

A reasonable PE ratio: Usually demand from investors pushes up the price of growth stocks so much that their PE ratios are well above the level for the market overall. It's not unusual for many growth stocks to sell at PEs two to three times that of the market, or even higher in some cases. The lower the PE you pay for a given level of earnings, the more money you stand to make. If possible, try to find growth stocks with PE ratios no higher than their projected earnings growth rates. So if a company's earnings are expected to rise 20 percent a year, you would ideally want to buy it for a PE of 20 or less. You won't always be able to meet this standard, but the closer you can get to it, the greater your chances of making money.

What to Look Out For in Growth Stocks

Unsustainable earnings growth: Investors are typically buying growth stocks on the basis of projected earnings. A stock that misses earnings or projections by a few cents a share can see its price drop 5 percent or more in a single day. And if the shortfall is more severe, the price can nosedive. After Oxford Health Plans revealed huge billing problems in October 1997 that would hurt revenues and profits, the company's stock plummeted nearly 63 percent in a single day.

Overpaying for the stock: The biggest downside to growth investing is that the stocks get too damn popular. When that happens, their prices can get bid up to such insane levels that falling short of expectations by even a slim margin can seriously dampen the stock's future appreciation potential or trigger a slide in its price.

JUST SAY NO TO IPOS

Many investors believe the "big money" is made in IPOs (initial public offerings). That's because when companies first make their stock available to the public, the price of those shares often soars quickly. After Internet browser company Netscape went public in 1995, for example, its shares almost tripled in value within six months.

But IPO profits can be illusory. For one thing, the hottest IPOs often go only to brokerage firms' wealthiest clients or, in a process called *spinning,* to executives at firms that investment bankers are wooing for business. In a sense, it's a rigged game.

Regular investors like you and me can get into IPOs. But the ones we're invited to buy are usually initial offerings of small companies with dubious prospects that are pitched by sleazy brokerage firms that manipulate share prices. This game is also rigged.

If that's not enough to deter you, consider this: The prices of many IPOs sag within a year, and within a few years the majority trail the market averages. After peaking in 1996, for example, Netscape's stock dropped almost 70 percent by late September 1998.

Yes, big money can be made in IPOs. But much of it is made by insiders at the expense of small investors who don't realize the risks they're taking. So if a broker calls claiming that IPO stands for "instant profit opportunity," just tell him it can also mean "it's probably overpriced."

BARGAIN HUNTING FOR UNDERVALUED STOCKS

While growth investors glom on to the most popular stocks, value investors are contrarians looking for bargains that the crowd has missed. So if you're the kind of person who heads straight for the discount-price CD bin at your local music store or who stocks up on clothing at season-end clearance sales, you might have the temperament of a value investor.

Value investors look for stocks that are selling for less than their true worth on the basis of one or more factors, such as their earnings power, the value of their underlying assets, or their cash flow. Some renowned value investors, such as Warren Buffett, the Omaha billionaire, look for stocks that are selling below what he calls their *intrinsic business value,* essentially what a smart and informed buyer would pay for the entire enterprise.

What makes value investing difficult is that concepts like "true worth" and "intrinsic business value" are difficult to pin down. Analysts can turn to a number of statistical measures in their search for undervalued stocks—ones selling at low price-earnings ratios and low price-to-book value ratios, for example—but these statistical measures can be misleading. A cheap price alone doesn't constitute a bargain. Just because a stock is selling at a low PE ratio doesn't mean it's a buy, any more than a $1.99 CD of *Barry Manilow Sings Christmas and Hanukkah Favorites* is a great deal. So a value investor must home in not only on stocks that are underpriced, but on ones that would be selling at a higher price if investors understood the stock better.

If you can identify truly undervalued shares, the rewards can be substantial—although you may have to wait as long as a few years before other investors see the hidden value and bid up the price of the stock. But over very long periods of time, value investors who choose wisely and wait patiently generally out-perform growth investors. What's more, because most value stocks are already selling at relatively depressed prices, they tend to hold up a bit better when the overall stock market falls. In my opinion, this combination of superior long-term returns and lower volatility makes value stocks the better buy.

What to Look For in Value Stocks

Low PE ratios: One possible sign of an undervalued stock is a dividend yield well below the average for similar stocks—say, 25 percent or more. Essentially, the low PE is telling you that investors overall don't think much of the company's future earnings prospects. If you're right and the other investors are wrong, then eventually the stock's PE should rise to the level of its peers, giving you a nice gain.

Low price-to-book ratios: If a company's price-to-book ratio per share—essentially the company's book value or net worth divided by shares outstanding—is well below that of similar stocks, you're essentially buying a piece of what the company owns at a price lower than what you would pay for similar assets in other firms. Ideally you would like to find stocks that are actually selling *below* their book value. That's a tough hurdle, though, especially in a thriving stock market.

What to Look Out For in Value Stocks

Stocks that are basically just dogs: It's easy to find stocks whose prices have been beaten down. Many newspapers run lists of stocks that have hit new lows, and services like Value Line publish lists of stocks with low PEs and price-to-book ratios. But just as a cigar is sometimes just a cigar, so too a cheap stock is sometimes just . . . a cheap stock that deserves to sell at a depressed price. If it's a technology stock, its software could be outdated; if it's a bank, its loan portfolio could be in big trouble. In other words, cheap doesn't automatically translate as "undervalued."

DON'T GET SUCKED INTO THE TRADING TRAP

Discount brokers have been engaged in an all-out price war the past few years, pushing brokerage commissions as low as $8 per trade if you buy and sell on the Internet or $12 via touch-tone phone. Those rates may drop even more in the future.

But you would be making a big mistake to trade more just because it seems cheaper than ever before. Here's why:

First, commissions aren't your only trading expense. Although you might not know it, you also incur a cost known as the *spread,* which is the difference between the "bid" (the price at which a broker will buy your stock) and the "ask" (the price at which a broker will sell you stock). In small stocks the spread can be substantial, often 3 percent or more of the value of the trade. The more you buy and sell, the more that spread acts as a drag on your returns.

Second, a study by University of California professors Terrance Odean and Brad Barber suggests that the more you trade, the less you earn, largely because increased trading boosts transaction costs. When Odean and Barber examined the brokerage accounts of 60,000 households from February 1991 through December 1996, they found that the most active traders earned 5.3 percentage points a year *less* than the average for all the households. "Our central message," concluded the authors, "is that trading is hazardous to your wealth."

So ignore the siren song of low brokerage commissions. The more you trade, the more likely you are to enrich a broker rather than yourself.

Stocks in need of a dramatic turnaround: Many investors confuse value investing with buying depressed stocks that require a reversal of fortune. Although the two strategies are somewhat related, there's also a big difference between the two. With a value stock, the company should be worth more on the basis of what is there now. In other words, you're saying investors are miscalculating the company's true worth today. In a turn-around situation, you are counting on some catalyst such as a new CEO or business plan to improve a company's future prospects. That is a much more risky undertaking. If the planned turnaround is less successful than you anticipate or it fizzles completely, the stock could be drubbed even more.

WHEN TO UNLOAD A STOCK

Ideally you want to buy and sell stocks as infrequently as possible. More trading means more commissions and a greater chance of making mistakes—in other words, selling good stocks and buying losers. And if you've got a gain in a stock you're unloading—and you're not dealing with a tax-advantaged account like an IRA or 401(k)—you'll also have to pay taxes when you sell. The bigger the tax bite, the less you'll have to reinvest in a new stock. Which means to come out ahead, the replacement stock you buy will have to do a lot better than your old one just to recoup brokerage commissions and the money you handed over to the tax man.

Still, there are times when you have to part ways with a stock. While there's certainly no foolproof set of rules I can give you that says when you should hold or fold on a stock, I can offer these three situations in which you should at least consider selling:

1. THINGS HAVE GONE TOO WRONG. If something has changed for the worse since you bought—the long-term earnings outlook has worsened considerably, the company has gotten into new businesses in which it has little experience, it's merged with another firm you're not anxious to be affiliated with—then you should reevaluate the stock with an eye toward selling. Be careful, though. You don't want to jettison a good stock if the problems appear temporary. Focus on the long-term prospects.

2. THINGS HAVE GONE TOO RIGHT. Sometimes after you've bought a stock, the rest of the world finally discovers it—and drives its price to insane levels. This happens regularly to value investors. The question then becomes "Is there still enough upside in me given its current price?" If you feel that the price is so bloated that the chances for decent gains over the next five years or so have been seriously compromised, consider selling. Remember, though, to factor in the tax you might have to pay on any gain on the sale.

3. THE STOCK'S GOTTEN TOO BIG FOR YOUR BRITCHES. Another downside of successful stock picking is that a big winner can wind up representing too big a piece of your portfolio. That can be dangerous, since a large portion of your wealth is then riding on just one stock. Generally, no stock should represent more than 10 percent of your overall stock holdings. If you get above 20 percent, you're really getting into the danger zone. If any of your stocks climbs above the 10 percent level, you might want to sell some shares to pare back your position.

MORE THAN YOU EVER WANTED TO KNOW ABOUT BONDS

If you're going to invest in bonds or bond funds—and I think virtually every investor should for reasons outlined in chapter 7—it's important that you understand a bit about how bonds work. They may seem like tame investments suitable for widows, wimps, and know-nothings. But people can and do get burned, sometimes badly, in bonds.

Basically there are two risks you've got to be aware of when investing in bonds: credit risk and interest rate risk. Here's the skinny on both of them:

CREDIT RISK. When you buy a bond, you are lending money to an issuer such as a company, a city, or the U.S. government in return for their promise to repay interest and principal on time. Credit risk measures the likelihood that the bond issuer turns out to be a deadbeat and welshes on that debt.

That risk varies, of course, depending on who issued the bond. U.S. Treasuries have zero credit risk. Uncle Sam will make good on his obligations, even if he has to jack up your tax rate or run the U.S. mint printing presses night and day. The chances of a big blue-chip company defaulting on one of its corporate bonds are also pretty low, although as you get into smaller companies or ones that are struggling financially, the risk of default rises. Even the mightiest companies can run into financial setbacks, however, in which case their bonds may become riskier. As for municipal bonds, the credit risk depends on the fiscal health of the state or local government issuing the bond.

Most investors, including professionals, look to the ratings assigned by research firms like Standard & Poor's and Moody's Investors Service to assess the credit risk of bonds. As you would expect, the lower the bond's rating, the more interest the issuer has to pay to entice investors to take on the higher risk involved in owning the bond. So you can definitely grab a higher yield by investing in riskier bonds, but, of course, the odds increase that you might get stiffed.

INTEREST RATE RISK. To understand interest rate risk, all you've got to do is think of a seesaw with interest rates at one end and bond prices at the other. If interest rates go up, bond prices go down. If rates go down, bond prices go up.

The reason behind this seesaw effect is simple. Let's assume you bought a newly issued thirty-year U.S. Treasury bond for its face value of $1,000 when the going interest rate on long-term bonds was 6 percent. And let's say that a month or so after buying it, long-term interest rates jumped up a percentage point, so that thirty-year Treasury bonds with a $1,000 face value now carry a coupon rate of 7 percent (which means they pay 7 percent, or $70 a year, for each face value of $1,000 versus $60 for the 6 percent bond).

Now suppose you wanted to sell your 6 percent bond. You can't change the interest rate on the bond itself. The rate is fixed, which is why bonds are often referred to as *fixed-income investments*. And clearly, anyone with $1,000 to pay for a bond would now much rather own one that pays $70 a year than $60 a year. So to convince someone to buy your 6 percent bond, you would have to offer it at a price far enough below $1,000 to compensate him for the lower interest payments. If interest rates rose another percentage point to 8 percent while you were deciding whether or not to sell your bond, its price would fall even further, since your bond would now have to be low enough to attract investors who can get 8 percent, or $80 a year, on new bonds. The more interest rates rise, then, the more bond prices fall.

But there's one other element to this process that determines how far your bond's price will drop when rates rise—namely, the seesaw's length, or in the case of bonds, the bond's maturity.

Generally, the longer the maturity of a bond, the higher the interest rate the bond pays. That's because when you buy a bond with a long term, say, thirty years, there's a substantial risk that you could be locked in to low interest payments for a long time if interest rates rise after you've bought the bond. If you buy a bond with a shorter term, say, five years, you're taking less risk because you can get stuck with a subpar rate of interest for only five years. So to entice buyers to take the higher risk inherent in long-term bonds, issuers generally have to pay investors a higher rate of interest. (There are rare occasions when long-term bonds pay less than short-term bonds, usually before a recession, but we needn't get into that here.)

The higher risk of a long-term bond is reflected in how much its price drops when interest rates rise. If you own a thirty-year bond and try to sell it after rates rise, the price has to come down substantially to compensate the buyer for taking lower interest payments for three decades. For example, a one-percentage-point jump in rates can result in a loss of 10 percent or so in a thirty-year bond. If the bond has a shorter term, say, five years, the loss may be only a few percentage points.

So the longer the seesaw—that is, the longer the maturity of the bond—the more prices fall when interest rates rise. Of course, seesaws go up and down, as do bond prices. So if you own a bond and interest rates fall, the price you would get for selling the bond would go up because the buyer would be getting higher interest payments than those on newly issued bonds.

If we could foretell the path of interest rates in advance, then obviously we would buy long-term bonds just before rates fell and shift to short-term bonds just before rates rose. Unfortunately no one can predict the future path of interest rates, not even the mighty Fed chairman Alan Greenspan. He can influence rates, but ultimately the buying and selling of thousands of investors in the bond market determine the level of interest rates. Given that unpredictability, I recommend sticking with intermediate-term bonds (those that mature in five to ten years) or short-term bonds (those that mature in two to five years). You won't get quite as much interest on these as you can on longer-term issues. But if rates rise, the prices of the bonds (or bond funds) you own won't be decimated—and you won't be stuck with subpar interest payments for as long a time as you would with long-term bonds.

YOUR MENU OF BOND CHOICES

Here's a rundown of your main choices when it comes to bonds. Even though you can buy individual issues of all the bonds described here, frankly, the only ones I think you should even *consider* buying on your own are Treasury bonds and, possibly, municipal bonds. I say "possibly" muni bonds because investors get lousy prices on municipal bonds when they buy in small amounts. So I wouldn't buy munis unless I had at least $50,000 to spread out over five different bond issues and I planned to hold the bonds till they matured.

As for the other types listed, in my opinion they're either too risky or too difficult for individual investors to evaluate. My suggestion is just do without them or buy them through a mutual fund.

U.S. GOVERNMENT IOUS—U.S. TREASURY BONDS: Treasuries come in four basic varieties: Treasury bills (aka T-bills), which mature in less than a year; Treasury notes, which mature in one to ten years; Treasury bonds, which mature in ten to thirty years; and a relatively new addition, Treasury inflation protected securities (TIPS), essentially Treasury bonds that guarantee you a rate of return over the inflation rate as long as you hold the bond to maturity.

If you're looking for a completely safe stash for the part of your portfolio you plan to devote to bonds, then Treasuries, which are backed by the full faith and credit of the U.S. government, are your best option. Treasuries also have another advantage: The interest they pay is exempt from state and local taxes, which effectively boosts their return relative to bonds with interest that is fully taxable.

But just because there's virtually no risk of the U.S. government defaulting doesn't mean that you can't lose money in Treasuries. Just like any other bond, Treasuries drop in value when interest rates rise.

BELLES OF THE BOND WORLD—GINNIE AND FANNIE MAES: Although their names may conjure up images of the wholesome girl next door, Ginnie Maes and Fannie Maes are actually mortgage-backed securities. Translation: They're essentially bonds that are backed by pools of home mortgages. Ginnie Maes are issued by the Government National Mortgage Association (GNMA, hence Ginnie Mae), while Fannie Maes are issued by the Federal National Mortgage Association (FNMA, or Fannie Mae). Although both these organizations were chartered by Congress, neither is technically a U.S. government agency, which means their securities aren't guaranteed by the U.S. government. As a result, they usually pay slightly higher rates than U.S. Treasuries. They also require higher minimum investments—usually $25,000 or more—although individual investors can also buy Ginnies and Fannies through mutual funds that invest in these and other mortgage-backed securities.

Still, I don't think Ginnie Maes and Fannie Maes are generally a good buy, despite the slightly higher rates they pay. That's because they give you all the downside of bonds with very little upside. If interest rates go up, Ginnies and Fannies lose money like any other bond. But if rates head down, their prices don't rise, as is the case with other bonds. The reason is that when interest rates fall, homeowners refinance their high-rate mortgages. When that happens, owners of Ginnie Maes get back the money that had been invested in those high-rate loans and must reinvest it in new mortgages paying lower rates. Unless you consider yourself pretty handy at forecasting the future direction of interest rates, I don't think Ginnies and Fannies offer enough upside to make up for the potential downside.

CORPORATE BONDS—INVESTMENT-GRADE AND JUNK: Thousands of U.S. companies issue bonds, usually as a way to finance growth in their business. If a rating agency like Standard & Poor's or Moody's Investors Service judges that the company will have no trouble making the interest payments and repaying principal on schedule, then the bond typically gets an investment-grade rating. Even the highest-rated corporate bonds, however, aren't as secure as Treasuries, so investment-grade corporates must pay a slightly higher rate of interest than Treasuries. Usually the difference in rates between investment-grade corporates and Treasuries runs anywhere from a half to a full percentage point.

If the rating agencies believe the company could run into trouble making interest and principal payments on a bond, they give the issue a below-investment-grade rating. Although some investment advisers prefer the euphemistic term *high-yield bond* when talking about below-investment-grade issues, these bonds are typically called *junk bonds*. Bonds can also start out with an investment-grade rating and be downgraded later because the company missed a payment or because its financial condition deteriorated. Bonds that slip from the investment grade to the junk heap are known as *fallen angels*. Since junk bonds are inherently more risky than investment-grade issues, they must pay higher rates of interest, usually anywhere from two to four percentage points above the rate on investment-grade issues.

TAX-FREE BONDS—MUNICIPAL BONDS: Muni bonds are issued by state and local governments or their agencies—local housing or bridge and tunnel authorities, water and sewer departments, that sort of thing. Their main appeal—make that their *only* appeal—is that they pay interest that's exempt from federal taxes and, if you're a resident of the state that issued the bond, free of state taxes as well. In a few cases munis are triple tax-exempt—free of federal, state, and local taxes.

Because of this tax-free status, munis carry lower rates of interest than taxable bonds. Still, if you're in the 28 percent or higher federal tax bracket, chances are that the yield on munis will be higher than the yield after taxes on a taxable bond.

Even though munis are issued by state or local governments or their affiliates, they are *not* as secure as Treasuries. Although it's relatively rare, munis do default. In one famous case, bonds issued by the Washington Public Power Supply System (WPPSS) defaulted in 1983, making them forever known as "WHOOPS" bonds. If you do decide to buy munis on your own, diversify into at least five issues (preferably not all in your home state), and stick to ones with the highest ratings from issuers like Moody's

Investors Service and Standard & Poor's or ones that carry municipal bond insurance.

CHOOSING A DISCOUNT BROKER

When you're buying individual securities, it pays to keep trading costs to a minimum. You have a better chance of doing that if you do business with a discount, rather than a full-service, broker. True, discount brokers aren't going to bombard you with investment ideas the way a full-service broker does. But I consider that a plus, since many of the "ideas" full-service brokers tout are nothing more than the recommended list of their firm or, worse yet, stocks that the firm holds in inventory and is looking to unload.

But while discount brokers offer substantial savings compared with full-service stock jockeys, you should be wary of choosing a discounter solely on price. Some discounters may be difficult to reach by phone. That can be a drag if you have questions or problems you don't want to talk about via e-mail. Others may take their sweet time in confirming trades. Still others may nick you for additional services.

If you stick with large established discounters like Charles Schwab and Fidelity, you won't get the lowest rates. But you'll probably get decent service and the security of knowing you're dealing with a firm that has a reputation to protect. You can lower your commissions dramatically by going to smaller firms that trade mostly on the Internet. But if you do that, you might want to do a bit more research first. The Online Investing Services site (www.sonic.net/donaldj) run by Don Johnson (no, not the *Miami Vice* guy; this DJ is a retired business professor) provides scads of information that can help you pick the best discounter for the way you trade. The site also has links to other sites that can help.

Following are ten well-known discount brokers that allow you to make trades through their Internet sites, over a touch-tone phone system, or by dealing with a broker (usually by phone). All of these firms also offer free stock quotes and various kinds of research at no charge through their Web sites. Because brokerage commissions change so frequently these days—usually heading down—I haven't included their prices. But you can check out their rates by calling them or clicking on their Web sites:

Ameritrade:	800-454-9272; www.ameritrade.com
Charles Schwab:	800-435-4000; www.schwab.com
Datek Online:	888-463-2835; www.datek.com
DLJdirect:	800-825-5723; www.dljdirect.com
E★ Trade:	800-786-2573; www.etrade.com
Fidelity:	800-544-7272; www.fidelity.com
National Discount Brokers:	800-888-3999; www.ndb.com
Quick & Reilly:	800-837-7220; www.quickwaynet.com
Waterhouse:	800-934-4410; www.waterhouse.com

HOW TO BUY STOCKS (AND BONDS) WITHOUT PAYING BROKERS' COMMISSIONS

If reducing brokerage commissions by dealing with a discounter appeals to you, then you'll probably love the concept of eliminating commissions entirely. But short of stiffing your broker, is there a way to pull off this feat? Yes. Let's start with stocks.

Today you can buy stock directly from more than 1,500 companies by setting up a *DRIP* or *DSP*—that is, a *dividend reinvestment plan* or *direct stock purchase plan*. To enroll in a DRIP, you usually must already own at least one share of the company's stock. Once you meet that condition, however, the company will automatically reinvest dividends in additional shares. Many DRIPs also allow you to purchase additional shares on your own directly from the company as well. With a DSP you can buy your first shares from the company, although many firms require an initial minimum investment of about $250 or so. After that, most DSPs will reinvest dividends in additional shares. Some companies will even sell you the shares at a 3 percent to 5 percent discount to the market price.

While you avoid brokerage commissions, you usually don't get a free ride in DRIPs and DSPs, however. Many plans may charge you $5 to $10 to enroll, and some also levy fees of $1 to $5 or so whenever you buy additional shares or sell shares. Many firms also assess you a portion of the brokerage fee the company pays, although that amount is usually less than you would pay on your own. Because of the welter of possible fees, you should always calculate what it's going to cost you to invest through one of these plans and compare that cost with what you would pay through a discounter. For example, Gillette charges a $10 enrollment fee plus a $5 charge for each cash investment and $.08 per share. (The company also levies a $1.25 charge plus $.08 per share to reinvest quarterly dividends.) That means that, not including the onetime enrollment fee, you would pay $13 each time you buy one hundred shares of Gillette stock. You would be better off buying those one hundred shares through any number of Net brokers.

Since the roster of DSPs and DRIPs consists mostly of large dividend-paying blue-chip firms—and particularly lots of banks and utilities—I don't think you can create a diversified portfolio of DSPs and DRIPs alone. But if you can find a handful of good companies that allow you to make regular investments and reinvest dividends at low fees, enrolling in a DRIP or DSP is an excellent way to practice dollar-cost averaging with individual stocks. For the names of companies that offer DRIPs and DSPs as well as their fees, you can check out the *Guide to Dividend Reinvestment Plans* ($25; Temper of the Times Communication, 800-388-9993). You can also learn more about the details of investing through DRIPs and DSPs—and even sign up for some plans—by visiting these Web sites: www.dripcentral.com, www.dripinvestor.com, and www.netstockdirect.

YOU'VE GOT AN UNCLE IN THE BOND BUSINESS

While you can't buy bonds directly from a company—and even if you could, I doubt you would want do—you can avoid brokerage sales commissions on Treasury securities by dealing directly with Uncle Sam, specifically the U.S. government's Treasury Direct program. In fact, in August 1998 the Treasury Department announced two changes that will make this long-standing program even more accessible to individual investors. First, the Feds reduced the minimum investment on Treasury bills and Treasury notes from $10,000 and $5,000, respectively, to $1,000. (The minimum on bonds had already been $1,000.) Second, the Treasury Department said that beginning in September 1998 investors would be able to buy Treasuries via computer by logging on to the Bureau of Public Debt's Web site (www.publicdebt.treas.gov).

For details on how to set up a Treasury Direct account, call your local Federal Reserve Bank or branch listed in the Yellow Pages or click on the Bureau of Public Debt Web site.

TRUE CONFESSION: HOW I PROVED MYSELF A STOCK MARKET GENIUS AND A DUNCE AT THE SAME TIME

I opened this chapter in a spirit of full disclosure, and I'd like to end it the same way. So I thought I would regale you with a story about my own investing experience. I realize that I'm taking the risk of blowing my credibility in telling you this story. After all, the "experts" aren't supposed to make errors. The truth is, however, that anyone who invests will eventually make mistakes— the key is to keep them to a minimum and learn from them. So here's my tale of investing prowess, pride—and my humbling fall . . . all rolled into my dealings with one stock: Berkshire Hathaway, the investment holding company run by Warren Buffett, one of the world's savviest investors and a billionaire to boot.

I had come to appreciate Warren Buffett after I interviewed him for a story I wrote in *Money* magazine back in the fall of 1987. Although he had already established himself as one of the best investors in history, he still had this folksy down-home aw-shucks manner that's the exact opposite of the kind of blowhard braggadocio you usually run into on Wall Street. Then again, Buffett operates out of Omaha, Nebraska, so maybe that has something to do with his self-effacing midwestern style.

Rather than try to amaze me during this interview with examples of his investing acumen, he talked about a relatively simple strategy of finding good solid companies selling for less than their true value and holding them for the long term: "If you can find companies that you want to be an investor in for five or ten years, you'll probably do reasonably well." To my surprise, he also claimed that he didn't own either a calculator or a computer—"or an abacus." He described his way of valuing companies as trying to figure out what their businesses are worth and then dividing by the number of shares outstanding. Buffett had applied this straightforward style of looking for value—an approach he had learned from another renowned value investor, the late Columbia Graduate School of Business professor Benjamin Graham—at the investing partnership he launched in 1956 and at Berkshire Hathaway, which he acquired in 1967.

Occasionally I would consider buying shares of Berkshire, but one thing stopped me: their steep price. Back before the October 1987 crash, Berkshire was trading at a virtually unheard-of price of $6,000 a share.

But after the stock market's meltdown in October 1987, I saw that Berkshire was trading at $3,050 a share. That was still a lot of money to put out for one share of stock. But considering that I was getting the services of perhaps the world's greatest investor, it seemed like a bargain. I summoned my courage—and my meager resources—and bought two shares for $6,100.

Now that I had my money riding on Warren, I began frequently checking Berkshire's stock price in the paper. And, to my utter delight, Berkshire shares began to climb. At this point I'm thinking two things to myself: What a genius I am for spotting this bargain, and What an idiot I was for not buying more.

Within seven months Berkshire Hathaway was selling at $4,000 a share. I was ecstatic—$4,000 a share! I was up 31 percent in just seven months! Was I not displaying Buffett-esque skills in my own investing? I began regaling friends, colleagues, and my wife with the story of how I had snapped up Berkshire shares at a steal and was now riding them to Buffett-like gains. And it all seemed so easy. Well, when you've got it, you've got it, I figured. And I obviously had it.

Then a little voice in the back of my head began whispering to me, *You've made 31 percent in just over half a year . . . you've got a $1,900 profit. Why not sell and lock it in?* At first I resisted. After all, one of the cornerstones of Buffett's investing philosophy is investing for the long term. Hadn't the master told me himself that you should look for companies you could hold on to for five to ten years? Hadn't he held on to some of his investments even longer, like the Washington Post shares he bought in 1973 and still owns? Wouldn't I be committing a sacrilegious act by investing in the company run by the ultimate long-term buy-and-hold investor and then selling it in *seven months?*

But the little voice wouldn't go away. It began saying things like *Sell. This stock* can't *go much higher. Who's going to pay more than $4,000 for one share of stock? It's absurd. Get out with a profit while you can.*

The voice won. I sold at $4,100 a share, netting a profit of $1,808 after brokerage commissions and thinking I had proven myself quite the astute investor.

As I write this in November 1998, a bit over ten years after selling, Berkshire has been trading at $64,500 a share. It had even climbed to $84,000 a share in June 1988. (Buffett has also issued additional Berkshire shares—typically called Baby Berkshires— that sell at a fraction of the price of the original shares.)

What a bonehead I was! If I had only held on instead of giving in to that whiny little voice in my head, as of November 1998 I would have been sitting on two shares of Berkshire worth $129,000—and a $122,900 profit. Enough to send my kid to college for maybe a year in 2010. To add insult to injury, the shares would actually qualify for the new low 20 percent capital gains rate. I wouldn't even have to share too big a part of my profits with the IRS.

So that's my tale of how, in one transaction with one investment, I proved myself to be a stock market genius and a fool. But at least I did learn a few lessons from this episode, which I share with you now:

1. BEWARE OF WHAT INNER VOICE YOU LISTEN TO. I realize now that the voice in my head urging me to sell was not the voice of investing reason. It was the voice of excitement and intrigue. Somewhere deep inside, most investors have a similar voice that tempts them to look at investing as a game that can be won and played again and again. Learn to ignore that voice.

2. DON'T BET AGAINST WARREN. What could I possibly have been thinking? On the one hand, here is a guy with a forty-year record of investing achievement who's created a fortune of several billion dollars for himself and billions more for his investors. And on the other hand is me, deciding whether to pull my piddling few thousand bucks away from him so I can reinvest the profits somewhere else. Hey, deciding whom to side with given that choice is a no-brainer. I should have stuck with Warren. After all, he'd already delivered me a $1,900 profit in just seven months.

3. DON'T BEAT YOURSELF UP TOO MUCH OVER MISTAKES. Okay, so I acted foolishly. I admit it. Then again, I could have done a lot worse. I could have sunk my six grand into real estate limited partnerships or specious insurance investments or bought $6,000 worth of Donny and Marie Osmond albums in the hopes they'll become hot collectibles one day. Admit your mistakes, learn from them, and move on.

CHAPTER 6

Investments You Can Just Say No To

• • • • • • • • • • •

In this chapter I'm going to make your job as an investor a lot easier. How? By ruling out entire categories of investments you can easily get by without.

The marketing departments of Wall Street brokerage firms and other financial services companies are continuously drumming up new investment products that, to hear them tell it, satisfy some gaping hole in investors' portfolios. So you're going to have brokers or planners explaining in serious tones why you really need commodities to protect you against unexpected spikes in inflation, or foreign currency funds to protect you against the unexpected decline of the U.S. dollar or gold bullion or Krugerrands to protect you against the unexpected end of civilization, when all financial assets will be worthless and only base metals, canned foods, and can openers will have any value. You'll also come across stories in magazines and newspapers telling you about obscure new little mutual funds—say, the

Carnivore-Vegetarian Fund, which invests half its portfolio in contracts for soybean meal and the other half in contracts for pork loins. No doubt there will be a chart showing how the investment *would have* fared over the past five years, had it actually been around five years ago.

But just remember: In the investing world, as in other endeavors, less is usually more. Piling your plate high with investments from Wall Street's smorgasbord is more likely to lead to financial indigestion than satisfying returns. And in the worst cases you could even fall prey to con artists and swindlers who are trying to wedge themselves between you and your money.

LEGITIMATE INVESTMENTS TOO COSTLY, COMPLICATED, OR FLAKY TO BE WORTHWHILE

There's nothing inherently wrong with the investments listed here. They all can do a certain job pretty well. And you could easily work them into a portfolio of stocks and bonds. Question is, do you really need them? I think not. Some are too complicated, others demand too much attention, and still others are illiquid and have high costs. To me, all this means that the benefits of owning them don't outweigh the hassle and risks.

WHY YOUR BEST OPTION IS TO AVOID OPTIONS

Over the past few years brokerage firms have begun pushing options on everything from individual stocks to stock market indexes like the Dow Jones Industrial Average and S&P 500—

even on mutual funds. An option is basically the right—but not the obligation—to buy or sell a security at a specified price within a specified time.

So, for example, if Coca-Cola shares were selling at, say, $65, and you believed they were ready to surge ahead, you could buy a call option with a strike price of, say, $75, which would give you the right to buy one hundred shares of Coke at $75 apiece for a given time, usually one to three months, although you can get options for longer periods. If Coke's stock rises in price, the value of your option rises as well. You can then sell the option for a profit, if you like. Or you can hold on longer. If Coke's price rises above $75 to, say, $85, you can sell the option for an even higher price, or you can exercise the option, in which case you get one hundred shares of Coke for $75, even though the market price is $85.

If you think Coke's price will fall, you can buy a put option, which gives you the right to sell Coke, in which case you could profit if the stock falls while you hold the option. You can also use options to protect profits you have in a stock. For example, if you owned Coke and were worried its stock price might drop, you could buy a put option. If Coke's price declined, the value of your stock would drop, but the value of your put option would rise, helping offset the loss on the stock.

All this sounds like an easy way to make money and protect your profits—which is exactly what the brokers and exchanges that trade options want you to believe. In fact, I think options are a waste of money for the vast majority of individual investors. Here's why: If you're buying an option because you believe a stock's price will rise or fall, you've got to be right about two things. You've got to predict which direction the stock will go, and you've got to get the time frame right as well, because the option is worthless once it expires. So in buying an option, you're removing time as an element in your favor. Of course, if you're right on both counts, you win big. Since each option controls one hundred shares of stock, you get more bang out of your investment, or *option premium,* which is the name for the price you pay for an option. But essentially, buying put or call options is the equivalent of betting black or red at the roulette table.

As for using options as a form of insurance to protect your profits, I don't see much value there, either. As insurance, options can be expensive. A put option good for two months that can be exercised at a price close to the stock's current market price—in other words, an option that would pretty much protect any profits you may have in a stock for as long as two months, even if the stock tanked—can cost roughly 4 percent of the value of the stock, not counting commissions of 2 percent or more of the cost of the option itself. You can get cheaper options, but they'll have a shorter life, or they'll have a lower strike price, which means you don't get to protect as much of your gain.

And when you think about it, what are you buying? Protection from a slump in the price of a stock. If you're a long-term investor, however, you shouldn't be worried about short-term dips in a stock's price. And if you're not investing for the long term—say, at least five years—then you shouldn't be in stocks anyway. So if a broker tries to sell you on options, claiming it's a strategy for sophisticated investors, just tell him you're more interested in finding simple ways to make money than complicated ways to lose it.

GOLDEN OPPORTUNITY—OR FOOL'S GOLD?

Back in the 1970s when the consumer price index was spiraling upward, gold, a traditional inflation hedge, was a dynamite investment. But after peaking at $850 an ounce in 1980, this precious metal hit $278 an ounce in January 1998, its lowest level in eighteen years. Could gold glitter again? It's possible. Gold is notoriously volatile, and investors have made money by buying at a low and selling after one of gold's periodic rallies. So even if it doesn't come close to regaining its 1980 peak—and virtually no one expects it to anytime soon—you can make money if you buy at a trough and sell during a rebound.

That's a big if. It's impossible to predict when these peaks and valleys will occur—and whether you own the metal itself, a gold stock, or a gold mutual fund, you're not likely to get any dividends while you're waiting for one of those upswings. If you want to speculate by playing the occasional bounces in the price of gold, that's fine. But you're speculating—a fancy name for gambling—not investing.

But what about the argument that your portfolio should always have a chunk of gold or gold stocks or mutual funds because the precious yellow metal provides a long-term hedge against inflation and also provides valuable diversification because gold prices move largely independently of stocks? That argument is sound, kind of. Gold generally does gain value when inflation ignites. And even though gold is a highly volatile investment whose value bounces up and down quite a bit, it can actually lower the volatility of a portfolio consisting of stocks and bonds. That's because gold has a low correlation to stocks, which means price spikes and troughs don't coincide with the bumps and grinds of stock prices. (For an explanation of correlation, see chapter 7.)

But the problem is that we haven't had much in the way of inflation scares since the early 1980s. So aside from occasional short-lived rallies, the returns on gold have been abysmal. So what would have happened had you followed the standard advice and in the beginning of 1988 put some of your money in a mutual fund that buys shares of gold-mining stocks and other precious metals–related investments and kept it there for ten years? You would have lost an annualized 3.6 percent a year for ten years. That's right, a *negative* 3.6 percent compounded annual return. If you have a hard time getting your mind around the concept of your money compounding at a negative rate, the following graph shows what would have happened to a $10,000 investment in the average precious metals fund for the ten years to January 1, 1998.

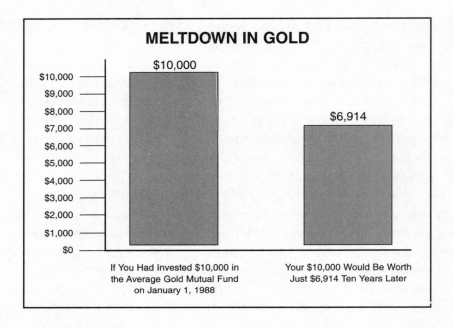

Could the next ten years be different? Sure. Maybe inflation will make a comeback and gold prices will rise and I'll be proved a nincompoop for telling you to ignore gold. But if you keep most of your long-term investment stash in stocks, chances are you will earn solid long-term returns that will keep your money growing faster than inflation—and you don't have to depend on a resurgence of inflation to reap those gains.

A REALISTIC LOOK AT REAL ESTATE

I'm not talking about your investment in your own home here. I consider that more a lifestyle decision than an investment. Instead I'm talking about buying a house or small apartment building that you would rent out to tenants. In telling you that you don't really need that kind of investment (or at least that you shouldn't even consider it until you've got a big chunk of money in a diversified portfolio of stocks and bonds), I know I'm going to offend the many fans of real estate investing, especially the guys who buy those infomercials you see at three A.M. that promise you can make a fortune buying for *no money down!*

But as I see it, the main problem with playing landlord is that it's incredibly time-consuming. Tenants are notorious for ringing you up late at night to complain about overflowing toilets or the hard-partying heavy-metal crowd in apartment 15D. Yes, you can hire a management company or on-site manager to take the flak and fix the problems. But that expense will eat into your return. And unless you've got a large investment portfolio beyond your real estate holdings, a rental property is likely to represent a very large portion of your net worth. Which would leave you financially vulnerable if the property's value doesn't appreciate well because, say, the neighborhood that looked up-and-coming a few years ago now looks down-at-the-heels.

Real estate aficionados will point out that there are several tax advantages to investing in real estate. If expenses such as depreciation, maintenance, and interest payments on the property's mortgage exceed rental payments, you can deduct up to $25,000 in losses per year against other income. But to do that, you've got to actively participate in managing the property. If your income (actually, your modified adjusted gross income; see a tax preparer or ask the IRS for a detailed explanation of this fractured phrase) exceeds $100,000, you lose $.50 of this write-off for each $1 of income above $100,000, and you can't take a penny of the loss against other income once your income hits $150,000. If you eventually sell the property, however, you can then use any losses you weren't able to deduct. I get a headache just thinking about all these complications—and I'm not even fielding those late-night irate calls from tenants.

Fact is, if you consider the equity you have in your home in relation to the value of the rest of your investments, chances are you already have all the exposure to real estate you need. But if you think you need more, then consider putting a small portion of your portfolio—say, 5 percent to 10 percent—into *real estate investment trusts* (*REITs*), which are essentially shares of companies that own commercial properties, or better yet, invest in mutual funds that specialize in REITs or companies connected to the real estate biz, which are offered by major fund companies like Vanguard, T. Rowe Price, and Fidelity. Investing in real estate funds or REITs will give you many of the benefits of real estate investing—though not the tax advantages—without the considerable hassles.

INSURANCE INVESTMENTS:
AS BAD AS THEY WANNA BE

When it comes to producing mind-bendingly complicated investments and then larding them with fees that drag down returns, insurance companies have few equals. Take variable annuities. The main selling point to variable annuities is that they offer the advantages of mutual funds—the chance to invest in a diversified portfolio of stocks and/or bonds—but with a tax advantage: your gains compound free of taxes until you pull out your money.

Problem is, two other features virtually cancel out the tax-deferral edge. First, most variables carry two layers of fees that siphon roughly *two percentage points a year* off your gross return. That's 30 percent to 100 percent more than most funds charge. Most also levy so-called surrender charges that zap you for as much as 7 percent of your account value if you pull your money out of the variable annuity in the first few years. Second, when you eventually pull your money out of the variable annuity, all gains are taxed at regular income rates. That means instead of paying a maximum capital gains tax rate of 20 percent, you can pay as much as 39.6 percent. That combination of high taxes and bloated fees often wipes out the advantages of tax deferral unless you're investing for fifteen to twenty years. It's just not worth it.

Insurance companies also like to tout the investment advantages of cash-value insurance policies, since they, too, allow gains to compound tax-deferred. And, agents point out, you can even make the gains tax-free by borrowing against the policy. But high fees erode insurance policy returns, too, starting with the fact that sales commissions and other marketing costs often eat up your entire first-year premium. As for the borrowing ploy to make returns tax-free, the downside is that if you let your policy lapse, those tax-free gains become taxable, which means you could be hit with a big IRS bill. If you need insurance—and most people do to provide income and pay off bills in the event a spouse dies—buy insurance. But don't mix insurance with your investment portfolio. If you do, you'll probably end up cheating yourself on both fronts—that is, you'll get less insurance than you need and lower investment returns than you can find elsewhere.

COLLECTIBLES MAKE EVEN INSURANCE INVESTMENTS LOOK GOOD

When you hear about the big scores—vintage Barbie dolls selling for thousands of dollars, original Honus Wagner baseball cards fetching more than half a million bucks at auction—it's easy to get the idea that you can buy up everything from 1960s *Monkees'* lunch pails to *Star Trek* memorabilia and then reap big profits when a wave of nostalgia-induced demand drives up the price of your collectibles years later. The problem: There's no way to know whether a period piece like an original Peter Frampton *Live!* album will be pursued by tomorrow's collectors or will be relegated virtually worthless to the trash bin of history. (Okay, so maybe in this case we know, but you get the idea.)

The other problem with collectibles is that they don't pay interest, dividends, or any other kind of ongoing return—unless, of course, you count the unalloyed joy of listening to your authentic Frank Sinatra porcelain figurine belt out "My Way" every time you tip Frank's fedora. The upshot: While you're waiting for the world to rediscover the romance of disco, you're earning *nada* on the thousands you invested in 1970s platform shoes and the original sheet music for the Hustle. So while accumulating every *Incredible Hulk* comic book published in the 1960s or collecting a matching set of Lady Di, Frank Sinatra, and Elvis commemorative plates may be a labor of love, as an investment venture it ranks as pure speculation. The same pretty much goes for art as an investment, by the way, except that you can make a much better case for having it hanging around the house, even if it doesn't generate decent returns.

WELCOME TO THE INVESTING HALL OF SHAME

Wall Street brokerages and other financial services firms aren't about to build a monument to the god-awful investments they've unloaded on their clients over the years. But that doesn't mean I can't create a little Museum of Investment Horrors right here. Take this quick tour of the four "rooms" portraying investing abuses of the past.

The Gallery of Limited Partnerships: Here you'll find examples of the limited partnerships that Wall Street firms pushed on thousands of naive investors in the seventies and eighties. Real estate limited partnerships take up most of the exhibit space, but stroll around, and you'll also find partnerships containing everything from windmill farms to jojoba bean plantations. The partnerships were sold as a tax dodge, with the added promise of double-digit returns. But the sponsors' big fees, as much as 10 percent of the cash going in, and other costs virtually assured "limited" returns at best. Investors lost millions in these dogs.

The Fake Private Pensions Exhibit: We've got ever-inventive life insurance companies to thank for this room. In the early nineties, private pensions were presented as a way for you to invest for retirement. In reality, the concept was a ruse. The private pensions were nothing more than cash-value life insurance policies that generated big commissions for the agents and fees for the insurer. Life insurers are more discreet now, but policies are still often sold using the lure of tax-deferred or even tax-free returns.

The Global Income Funds Exposition: With interest rates low in the late eighties and early nineties, fund-company marketing savants were desperate to find an investment that could generate lucrative fees and be pitched to investors as a place to get high yields with low risk. Their solution: short-term global income funds. These funds could take advantage of high interest rates being paid in other countries but also claim to be safe by sticking to government bonds. The idea worked, until rising interest rates and problems with the European exchange rate system whacked these "safe" funds for losses.

The Derivatives Display: This section is a favorite among income investors. In an attempt to boost yields in the early nineties, some bond funds began adding risky derivatives to their otherwise safe short-term government bond portfolios. The derivatives—essentially investments whose value is linked to an index or asset—worked fine as long as interest rates stayed low. But when rates inched up in 1994, their value plummeted. To their surprise and horror, many investors in short-term U.S. government bond funds were suddenly saddled with losses.

BEWARE THESE BOGUS PITCHES

Thousands of people lose millions of dollars in a variety of investment scams and schemes each year. The ruses come in all kinds of variations, but many revolve around themes such as the assurance of high but safe returns or the promise of an inside deal or a hot tip, these days often on the Internet. Here's a look at three typical pitches. If you hear these or anything remotely like them, you should assume you're the target of a scam, not just at the receiving end of a pesky sales spiel. Put your checkbook away, don't sign anything, hang up the phone, or just walk away. In short, don't invest a cent if you think there's the slightest chance you're being conned. For the names of securities regulatory agencies and other places to report such come-ons, see chapter 8.

"You'll earn guaranteed high returns on this investment—*and it's as safe as a certificate of deposit!"* Crooks know that investors are suckers for the combination of lofty returns and low risk. After all, what better way to gain investors' attention than to appeal to their greed for high returns while at the same time allaying their fear of losing money? So scamsters are always coming up with bogus investments that promise huge returns but also guarantee the protection of your principal. One variation on this theme that's lured millions of dollars from gullible investors in recent years is the sale of a fake investment that goes by the name *prime bank notes.*

Con artists peddling these bogus notes told investors that the notes paid returns of more than 100 percent a year in some cases and that they were backed by the World Bank, an organization based in Washington, D.C., that provides loans to underdeveloped countries. Of course, the notes were nothing more than a ruse to separate investors from their money. Once investors turned over their cash, the con artists running this scam handed over a fake note and disappeared with the investors' money.

Dressed up in any variety of convincing artifices, come-ons for bogus investments may at first glance seem to have a ring of authenticity. But if you pare away the pretenses and think about what's actually being offered, it pretty much always boils down to the promise of big returns with little or no risk—a combination that common sense tells us is impossible to achieve.

"Have I got a great inside tip for you!" Your phone rings, and within seconds a broker on the other end of the line is breathlessly describing what appears to be an incredible moneymaking opportunity in a stock you've never heard of: "I've got a situation here, an Internet stock called Nothing But Net, selling for $5 a share, that's going to be making an important product announcement in a few days. A *big* one. I've been following this stock for months, and I know it's gonna move as soon as this news is out. I'm talking $10, $15, maybe even $20 within a month. I'm going to start you out small with this winner, let's say a $5,000 investment, to gain your trust. And once you double or triple that five grand, we'll talk about even bigger deals. So let's open this account right now and make some money."

If you invest that five grand, someone's going to make money all right. But it won't be you. When you hear a spiel like this, you know you're the target of a cold-call touting penny stocks, basically a scripted sales pitch from a broker flogging worthless stocks that typically sell for $5 a share or less. Penny stock firms often manipulate the price of the companies they sell to give an investor a quick profit, but that's only so you'll buy more of that stock or another. And guess whose shares you're buying? The broker's or his firm's. When the brokers have sucked as much cash out of you and other clients as they think they can get, they let the stock fall to its natural level, which can be just cents a share. This kind of market manipulation has proved so profitable, there's evidence that organized crime families might even be getting into the penny stock act. ("I've got a great stock tip you can't refuse.")

The easiest way to avoid this scam: *Never* invest with a broker you haven't met face-to-face in his office, particularly if the broker is promising unrealistic gains. Even if the broker works for a company you're familiar with, you should always check out his background first with regulators.

"Check out this terrific stock that's making waves on the Internet!" The Internet has opened up huge vistas of information to investors. It's also made it a lot easier for crooks to drive up the price of a stock artificially by spreading rumors about what an outstanding buy it is. So if you frequent Internet investing chat rooms, bulletin boards, and forums, take care you don't fall for a ploy known as *the pump and dump,* which typically goes like this: A stock promoter who already owns lots of shares of stock in a tiny (often high-tech) company will begin touting the stock in cyberspace chat rooms or by sending e-mail to people who discuss investments online. Spurred on by the glowing reviews of the company and promises of big gains in the stock, investors begin buying shares, pumping up its price. Once the stock price has soared, however, the promoter dumps the shares he owns at a tidy profit, and the unsuspecting investors roped into this scheme suffer losses when the share price eventually crashes.

Of course, the pump and dump is hardly the only fraud you're likely to run across in cyberspace these days. Fake investments, phony online auctions, affinity frauds targeting specific ethnic and religious groups, and a variety of Ponzi schemes flourish on the Net. Securities fraud on the Internet has become so prevalent that in July 1998 the SEC announced it had formed a new unit, the Office of Internet Enforcement, to combat the problem. The new unit consists of just two people, however, so don't expect the Net's fraud busters to clean up cyberspace overnight.

Your best protection against becoming a victim of Internet fraud: Never invest solely on the basis of any information, tips, or advice you pick up in online chat rooms. Always check it out with several other sources. After all, the Internet provides a cloak of anonymity that makes it difficult to assess the motives of chat room participants. Usually the only thing you know for sure about your fellow chatsters are their screen names. So do you really want to buy or sell a stock or any other investment solely on the basis of the recommendation of someone who goes by the name MR HOT STOCK?

CHAPTER 7

Fix Your Mix

• • • • • • • • • • •

What Mom and Asset Allocation Have in Common

Remember those platitudes and nuggets of advice your mom spewed out what seemed like every ten minutes when you were a kid? Things like "Try to eat a fruit, a vegetable, and a starch every day" and "Put a hat on if you're going out in the sun" and the ever-popular "Just because your friends are acting like idiots doesn't mean you should act like a crazy person, too." And remember how it was only *after* you grew up that you realized Mom was usually right?

Well, let me play the role of Mom for a moment and impart some maternal investing wisdom: Instead of spending virtually all your time hunting for the next top-performing stock or mutual fund, put some time and energy into building a portfolio that contains several different types of investments that complement each other. That process of divvying up your investment holdings among a variety of investments—typically stocks,

167

bonds, and money-market funds—goes by the highfalutin name *asset allocation,* a six-syllable phrase that essentially means putting your eggs into a variety of baskets instead of just one.

Why focus on your overall portfolio when it's obviously the investments themselves that actually generate the returns? Two main reasons. First, it's virtually impossible to predict which specific investments will be winners in any given year. By spreading your dough around, you increase the chance that you'll have at least a bit of your money in a sector that is doing well, and you eliminate the risk of putting all or most of your money in a hot sector that may be on the verge of flaming out.

Second, owning a broad mix of investments often allows gains in one part of your portfolio to offset or at least dampen the effect of losses in another part of your holdings. I don't want to give you the impression that asset allocation can immunize your portfolio against losses. It can't. Although it's rare, sometimes many categories of investments do poorly all at once. In 1994, for example, both U.S. stock mutual funds and international stock funds as well as both domestic and foreign bond funds all lost money. But the point of asset allocation isn't to prevent losses altogether. The aim is to earn the returns you need to reach your financial goals while taking a level of risk that allows you to sleep at night.

THE ZIGZAG EFFECT

To get the best return for whatever level of risk an investor is willing to stomach, one of the factors investment advisers look at is the *correlation* among different types of assets. Correlation is the technical term for measuring how different assets fare versus one another over the course of varying market cycles. Security analysts measure the correlation between two assets—such as stocks and bonds, or two different types of funds—on a scale of 1.0 (which means the assets move exactly in synch over time) to -1.0 (the assets move in opposite directions).

According to fund-rating firm Morningstar, for example, domestic small-company growth funds have a correlation of approximately 0.62 to domestic large-company growth funds. And while foreign stock funds sometimes sink right along with U.S. shares—witness how many U.S. stocks and foreign shares both got hit in the wake of 1997's Asian crisis—over long periods of time they still tend to move fairly independently of the U.S. market, which is reflected in foreign stock funds' relatively low correlation of 0.44 to funds that buy large U.S. growth stocks.

By creating a mix of investments that are not highly correlated to each other—in other words, ones that might zig while others zag—you can create a portfolio that gives you an acceptable rate of return given the risk you're willing to assume. For example, if you had invested all your money in the stocks in the Standard & Poor's 500 index at the beginning of 1970, you would have earned a return of 12.9 percent over the next twenty-eight years. Of course, you would have had to suffer through a one-year loss of 39 percent and a worse quarterly loss of 43 percent. If, on the other hand, you had invested 70 percent of your money in a blend of S&P 500, small-company, and foreign stocks and put the remaining 30 percent in intermediate-term U.S. government bonds, you would have earned a still respectable 12.3 percent but cut your worst yearly loss to 27 percent and worst quarterly loss to just over 30 percent. So the goal in building a portfolio is to find a mix that provides the balance of risk and return that's comfortable for you.

HOW TO BECOME A MIX MASTER

Like most things in investing, arriving at a diversified portfolio can be an extremely complicated process or a relatively simple one. As you'd expect, most financial planners and other investment advisers who specialize in building portfolios take the complex approach, typically collecting variables like the correlation of different asset classes, their risk, and their estimated future returns and plugging them into a computer software program that then spews out dozens, hundreds, or even thousands of different portfolios with a variety of expected returns and levels of risk. If you want to go this route, you'll have to hire a financial planner or buy specialized asset allocation software. Many of the portfolios that planners and other advisers recommend can contain upward of a dozen or so funds and may also require selling funds and revising the basic mix of stocks and bonds in response to changing market conditions. Which means you'll probably have to hire a planner to keep track of your portfolio or spend a lot of time doing that yourself. Maybe all that time and effort will pay off in vastly superior returns. Or maybe not.

But if you're not inclined to pay a planner or buy expensive software—and you don't want to make an avocation of tending your portfolio—you can still reap many of the rewards of asset allocation by taking a streamlined approach. You won't be able to impress friends at parties by rattling off the correlations and standard deviations of the fifteen funds in your portfolio. Then again, you'll have time to go to parties because you won't always be in meetings with your financial planner.

My recommendation: Start with a very simple mix of stocks and bonds based on your financial goals and stomach for risk. Once you've got your basic allocation down cold, you can fine-tune it later by adding a wider variety of stocks or funds. Or if you feel less is more where a diversified portfolio is concerned, you can stick with a simple mix.

FIX YOUR MIX

To arrive at the blend of stocks and bonds that makes sense for you, first check out the four steps outlined here. Then use one of the three model portfolios that appear later in this chapter as a blueprint for constructing your own portfolio.

1. SETTLE ON YOUR INVESTING TIME HORIZON. The single most important factor in setting your portfolio mix is the number of years you have to reach your goal. If you're investing for the long term—say, to accumulate money for a retirement nest egg you won't tap into for another dozen years or more—then your main concern is making sure that your money grows faster than inflation so you can increase your purchasing power. Since stocks generally offer the best inflation-beating gains over very long periods of time, you should tilt your mix toward stocks, probably along the lines of the 70 percent stocks–30 percent bonds Aggressive Portfolio on page 179. A portfolio like this will take some big hits when stock prices drop. But you have plenty of time for your portfolio to bounce back.

If you are putting away money you'll need within a few years—say, to buy a car or house—then a portfolio heavily weighted toward stocks is probably too risky. If stock prices melt down, you could have a big loss in your portfolio just when you need your money. If the loss is big enough, you might have to postpone buying the car or house. The better course is to tilt your portfolio mix more toward bonds, as in the Conservative Portfolio on page 177, which has a mix of 30 percent stocks and 70 percent bonds. As you near your goal, you'll want to move more money out of stocks and put it into both bonds and money funds. By the time you're within a year of tapping your stash, virtually all your money should be in short-term bonds or money funds.

2. CONSULT YOUR GUT. Ultimately the mix of stocks and bonds you decide on has got to pass the "Can I sleep at night?" test. After you read this chapter, your head may tell you that as a long-term investor you should have a mix of, say, 70 percent stocks and 30 percent bonds. But if hearing about a five hundred-point free fall in the Dow Jones Industrial Average on the evening news triggers nightmares in which Maria Bartiromo's reports from the New York Stock Exchange floor include updates on the mounting losses in your portfolio, then you may have to ratchet back your stock allocation a bit. On the other hand, if you are investing for the long term, you don't want to wimp out and load up too much on bonds and money funds. Otherwise, when retirement arrives you could find yourself living a nightmare of trying to get by on a retirement stash that has lost purchasing power to inflation over the past twenty years.

3. DIVERSIFY, BUT DON'T OVERDO IT. You can get much of the risk-reducing benefit of a diversified portfolio by holding a very simple mix of just stocks and bonds. For example, a study by investment firm Neuberger & Berman found that someone who simply kept 70 percent of her money in S&P 500 stocks and 30 percent in five-year Treasury securities from 1960 through 1995 would have gotten 92 percent of the gains of an all-stock portfolio but with 25 percent less volatility. By branching out to include other types of investments, however, you may be able to increase your overall returns without drastically jacking up the risk of your portfolio. For example, within your overall stock allocation, you might include a dollop of small stocks or small-stock funds. Although big U.S. blue chips have led the market for most of the nineties, over long periods of time in the past small stocks have outperformed the big boys by a margin of one to two percentage points a year.

To prevent your returns from depending solely on the U.S. market, you might consider adding a foreign stock fund to your mix. U.S. investors have never wholeheartedly embraced international investing. In fact, studies of fund shareholders show that, on average, only about 20 percent to 30 percent of investors even bother to own foreign funds. What's more, the U.S. stock market has been so strong in the nineties that many investors figure they don't need to go beyond U.S. shores to find the best returns. That attitude is understandable. After all, for the ten years to January 1, 1998, foreign stocks overall gained just 6.6 percent annually, compared with 18.1 percent for the S&P 500 over the same period.

Before the U.S. markets took the lead in the mid- and late 1990s, however, foreign shares had been riding high for most of the 1980s and early 1990s. Which will lead for the next ten years? Neither I nor anyone else knows. But the U.S. market isn't likely to outrun foreign shares forever. And since U.S. and foreign shares tend to move independently of each other over the long term—they have "low correlation" in asset allocation lingo—adding a foreign stock fund can also help reduce the overall level of risk in your portfolio.

On the bond side of your portfolio, I think it pays to keep things simple. Intermediate-term U.S. government bonds, or bond funds, should pretty much do the trick, although if you're in the 28 percent or higher tax bracket, you may want to substitute high-quality tax-free municipal bonds or bond funds. One possible embellishment you might consider to bulk up returns in this part of your portfolio is a junk bond fund. Yes, the risk of default in junk bonds is much higher than for government bonds, where the chances of default are nil. But over the years the higher returns on junk have more than compensated investors for the increased risk. I wouldn't put all my bond money in the junk heap, but I don't consider it financially reckless to put a small percentage of your portfolio in a junk bond fund run by an established fund family like Vanguard, Fidelity, or T. Rowe Price.

One caveat: The more different types of investments you add to your portfolio, the more effort you'll have to put into keeping tabs on your holdings. More stocks and funds means more paperwork, more decisions, more potential for mistakes—and less time for enjoying life. In building a portfolio, as with many other things in life, less is more. So I advise you to keep it simple, even if it means giving up some return. Remember, your aim is to earn decent returns at a level of risk you can stomach, not to prove that you can squeeze every type of mutual fund known to man into one portfolio.

4. REBALANCE YOUR PORTFOLIO ANNUALLY.
Once you've decided on a mix, let it be. Many investment advisers recommend changing your allocations in response to market conditions. They've even come up with an impressive-sounding name for this practice: *tactical asset allocation*. Fancy name or not, I suggest you resist the urge to make any substantial shifts in your portfolio in reaction to the markets. Such moves are more likely to undo the benefits of asset allocation than they are to boost your returns. Instead you should simply let the various parts of your holdings rack up their gains or losses and then at the end of the year rebalance your portfolio. If the proportions in your portfolio haven't gotten severely out of whack, you can just add any new money you invest to whichever investments have lagged over the previous year.

But if one part of your portfolio has bulked up so much that adding new money can't restore the whole to a semblance of balance, then you should sell off some of your winners and put the proceeds into the laggards. Unless you're dealing with tax-deferred accounts like an IRA or 401(k), such sales will most likely trigger taxes. That's a drag, to be sure. But by selling investments that have appreciated in value and putting money into those that have trailed, you're keeping your portfolio on track, plus you're doing what many investment advisers preach but seldom practice—selling high and buying low.

BRING ON THE SUPER MODELS (MODEL PORTFOLIOS, THAT IS)

Now that you know a bit about the incredibly fascinating theory behind asset allocation and you've got a few tips on how to translate that theory to your own financial situation, you can start putting together your own portfolio.

To help you get started, I asked Bob Bingham, an investment adviser with the San Francisco firm Bingham, Osborn & Scarborough, to come up with three model portfolios that could serve investors trying to achieve a variety of different goals. Our aim was to make things easy but at the same time provide a flexible framework that would allow more adventurous investors to create portfolios with a broadly diversified group of investments. So think of these portfolios as starting points that you can tailor depending on how much work you want to put into investing, how much risk you're willing to take, and what kinds of returns you need to get to your goals.

If you really want to make things simple, you could pretty much stick to index mutual funds in the exact proportions outlined in the model portfolios. So, for example, if you are investing for a long-term goal such as retirement, you could put 30 percent of your money in a bond index fund such as Vanguard's Bond Index Intermediate-Term fund, 30 percent in a stock index fund like the Vanguard Index 500, another 20 percent in Vanguard Index Small Capitalization Stock, and 20 percent in a diversified international fund. If you find even that mix too complicated, you could jettison the small-cap and foreign stakes and simply put 30 percent of your money in the bond index fund and the other 70 percent in Vanguard Index Total Stock Market, a fund that mirrors the performance of both large- and small-company U.S. stocks.

On the other hand, if you're willing to do a little more work, you could branch out into asset classes not specifically listed in the model portfolios. You might consider adding a small dose of high-yield (aka junk) bond funds to the bond component of your portfolio or a value-oriented stock fund to the domestic stock portion of your holdings. If you're willing to ride out some horrendous downturns in hopes of getting bigger returns, you might even think of including an international emerging markets fund in the international portion of your mix.

You can also fine-tune these portfolios in a variety of ways to adjust the level of risk. Concerned that a 70 percent stock–30 percent bond mix is too wild for you, but fifty-fifty is too tame? Move to a 60 percent stock–40 percent bond mix. You can also dampen risk a bit in any of these portfolios by plugging some money-market funds into the bond portion of your portfolio. The bottom line: Feel free to experiment—you don't have to worry about being pulled over by the asset allocation police for breaking the rules.

Of course, you may have to adjust the proportions in your portfolio as you near the time when you need your money. For example, if you start out with the fifty-fifty Middle of the Road Portfolio on page 178 because you're investing for your child's college education ten years away, your portfolio should look more like the 30 percent stock–70 percent bond Conservative Portfolio on page 177 when your kid enters senior year in high school. And by the time your little scholar is entering the third year of college (assuming this is the third of four years), the money earmarked for college expenses should be invested in money-market funds and short-term bond funds.

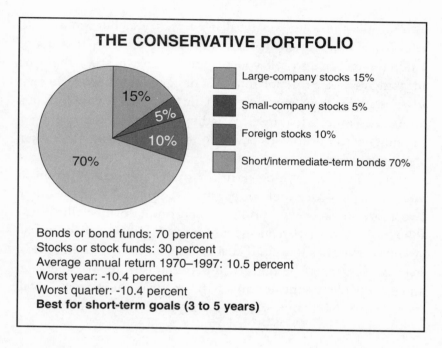

THE CONSERVATIVE PORTFOLIO

15%

5%

10%

70%

Large-company stocks 15%

Small-company stocks 5%

Foreign stocks 10%

Short/intermediate-term bonds 70%

Bonds or bond funds: 70 percent
Stocks or stock funds: 30 percent
Average annual return 1970–1997: 10.5 percent
Worst year: -10.4 percent
Worst quarter: -10.4 percent
Best for short-term goals (3 to 5 years)

If you're looking to invest money for a short period of time—say, you're accumulating a down payment for a house you'll buy within the next three to five years—you'd probably want to start with a mix something like the Conservative Portfolio shown here. The idea behind this bond–heavy mix is to give you a shot at higher returns than you would earn in money–market funds, a bank account, or bonds alone, but to avoid the risk of big losses by investing mostly in stocks. The stock portion of the portfolio is there to add a little oomph, to bolster your returns. And the big slug of bonds is meant to provide steadier, if somewhat smaller, returns, as well as a bit of ballast in case the stock market gets choppy. For example, even in the depths of the horrible 1973–1974 bear market, when the Dow Jones Industrial Average fell more than 40 percent, this portfolio never lost more than 10.4 percent of its value.

A portfolio like this one would have returned about 10.5 percent over the twenty-eight years from 1970 through 1997. (That assumes the portfolio was rebalanced each year but ignores the effect of transaction costs and taxes.) Astute reader that you are, I don't even have to tell you that this return figure is kind of meaningless, since this portfolio was designed for short-term savings, not long-term investing. And, in fact, even if you consider yourself a conservative investor, I think you would be making a big mistake to opt for this portfolio mix for anything other than short-term goals.

But I mention the long-term return of this portfolio to show you how much you would be giving up compared with the other two more stock-heavy options, which outperformed this portfolio by 0.9 and 1.8 percentage points a year, respectively, over that twenty-eight-year stretch. If that margin doesn't sound impressive, consider this: The difference between earning 10.5 percent and 12.3 percent annually on a $10,000 investment would total more than $16,000 over twenty-eight years, before taxes.

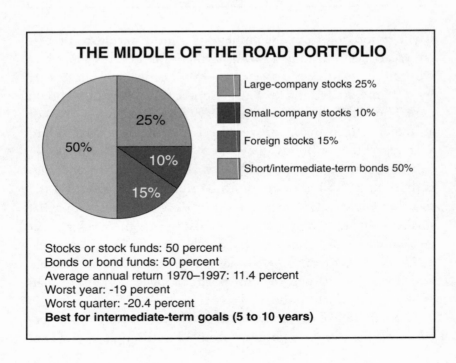

THE MIDDLE OF THE ROAD PORTFOLIO

- Large-company stocks 25%
- Small-company stocks 10%
- Foreign stocks 15%
- Short/intermediate-term bonds 50%

50% — 25% — 10% — 15%

Stocks or stock funds: 50 percent
Bonds or bond funds: 50 percent
Average annual return 1970–1997: 11.4 percent
Worst year: -19 percent
Worst quarter: -20.4 percent
Best for intermediate-term goals (5 to 10 years)

If you've got five to ten years to reach a goal, you can afford to sink more money into stocks in search of higher returns. Why? Because if you suffer a setback, you have a few years to recover and make up for losses before you start pulling money out of your stash. So, for example, if you are investing money for the college education of a child who's now just finishing grade school, you might start with a fifty–fifty mix like the one shown here, and gradually move closer to the mix in the Conservative Portfolio as Junior's enrollment date approaches.

Over longer stretches, the Middle of the Road Portfolio's bigger stock holdings should propel it to higher returns than the Conservative Portfolio. And, true to theory, this mix earned an average 11.4 percent annually from 1970 through 1997, outperforming the more wimpish conservative mix by 0.8 percentage points a year. But in return for those higher gains, you would have had to accept more risk. While the Conservative Portfolio

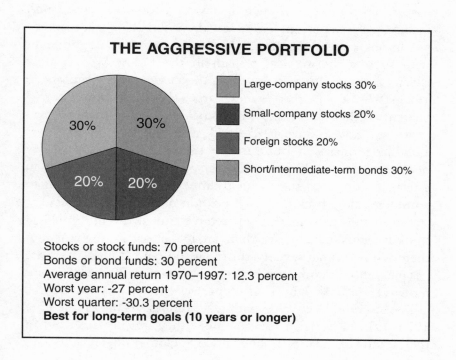

THE AGGRESSIVE PORTFOLIO

- Large-company stocks 30%
- Small-company stocks 20%
- Foreign stocks 20%
- Short/intermediate-term bonds 30%

Stocks or stock funds: 70 percent
Bonds or bond funds: 30 percent
Average annual return 1970–1997: 12.3 percent
Worst year: -27 percent
Worst quarter: -30.3 percent
Best for long-term goals (10 years or longer)

never dropped more than 10.4 percent over any year or quarter, the Middle of the Road mix was down as much as 20.4 percent during the 1973–1974 bear market. Still, as long as you have five to ten years before you have to begin drawing on your investments, a fifty-fifty mix like this is a reasonable way to grab decent returns without taking foolish risks.

If you're investing for a long-term goal such as retirement or future college tuition for a young child, then you don't have to worry about every little (or even big) dip in stock prices. Provided you don't panic and sell, you've likely got enough time to ride them out. Instead you should be making sure that over the long term the value of your portfolio grows even after adjusting for inflation and taxes. The surest way to do that: Put the majority of your money in stocks. The 70 percent stock–30 percent bond mix of this portfolio is a reasonable starting point.

Over the twenty-eight years from 1970 through 1997, this portfolio would have earned an average 12.3 percent, although it would have taken some gut-wrenching dives en route to those gains, including a 30.3 percent loss during the 1973–1974 bear market.

No one knows, of course, whether this portfolio might be hit with such withering losses again in the future. We certainly haven't seen anything approaching the ravages of the prolonged 1973–1974 bear market—where large stocks lost more than 43 percent of their value and small stocks fell more than 60 percent—since, well, since 1973–1974. Even the crash of 1987 was a blip by comparison. But if merely thinking about the *possibility* of a 20 percent to 30 percent loss makes you want to curl up in a fetal position and suck your thumb, then you might want to consider scaling back the stock portion of this portfolio a tad.

Given the stock market's incredible run in the mid-1990s, I think it's equally likely that there are lots of macho investors out there who consider seventy-thirty far too tame a mix. These are people who've come to believe that annual 20 percent-plus returns are a birthright. That it's perfectly normal for stocks like Yahoo! to double in value within six months. If they remember 1973–1974 at all, it's a hazy memory they quickly push out of their minds, like platform shoes, disco, and other unpleasant 1970s images. Their thought process goes something like this: *Stocks clearly generate the highest returns, so why drag my portfolio down with boring old bonds? Asset allocation is for academic eggheads and wimps. I'll go 100 percent stocks. If the market crashes, I've got the* cojones *to hang in until it rebounds.* Of course, the kinds of people you hear this sort of drivel from usually weren't investing in the early 1970s. So they never actually had to live through a period when large-company stocks lost 43 percent of their value in a single quarter and small stocks got hammered with a single-quarter loss of 60 percent. Ouch! And you can't help but wonder whether their macho bluster would fade in the face of such withering losses.

TOO BUSY OR TOO LAZY TO BUILD A PORTFOLIO? TRY A ONE-DECISION FUND

Despite my best efforts, I know that some people just won't go to the trouble to create even the simplest versions of the portfolios I've outlined in this chapter. And others may not have enough cash to make building a diversified portfolio worthwhile. If you fall into either of these groups, you could just let your money rot in a bank—or you could consider what I refer to as *one-decision funds,* funds that are their own little self-contained portfolios of stocks, bonds, and cash equivalents.

Typically, fund companies offer a variety of these portfolios, each designed for investors with different risk tolerances. When you're young, for example, you could start with an aggressive portfolio that might hold 80 percent in stocks and 20 percent in bonds and money-market securities combined, then switch to a moderate-risk portfolio of 60 percent stocks, 30 percent bonds, and 10 percent money-market securities, and then, after you're retired, move to a conservative portfolio that might have a mix of 40 percent stocks, 40 percent bonds, and 20 percent money-market securities. The fund manager can typically shift these allocations by as much as ten percentage points or so either way and also spread the stock and bond portions of the portfolio among U.S. and foreign issues. Among the fund companies offering such portfolios are T. Rowe Price (Personal Strategy funds), Dreyfus (Lifetime Portfolios), Schwab (Asset Director funds), and Vanguard (LifeStrategy funds).

If switching from one portfolio to another two times during your lifetime also strikes you as too much work, then consider one of the Wells Fargo Stagecoach LifePath funds. You pick from a menu of funds, depending on when you plan to start withdrawing your money. There's a portfolio for the year 2010, 2020, 2030, and 2040. The manager automatically shifts the mix from stocks to bonds as that date approaches, so you don't have to move from fund to fund. You do, however, have to pay a 4.5 percent sales charge on the amount you invest. The Fidelity Freedom funds follow a similar strategy—without the load—by investing in varying mixes of Fidelity stock, bond, and money funds.

Of course, by choosing an off-the-rack portfolio, you give up the right to tailor your holdings to your own tastes. But if it's a choice between a ready-made mix or none at all, then a one-decision fund beats nothing at all. Is that a ringing endorsement or what?

MEMO TO RETIREES: DON'T PIG OUT ON BONDS

Many investors in their sixties and seventies load up their port-folios almost exclusively with bonds or bond funds. Typically that's because retirees often look to their investment portfolio to provide current income, so bonds seem like a natural fit. Many older investors also gravitate toward bonds because they fear that the savings that took a lifetime to accumulate could be wiped out in a stock-market meltdown.

Fix Your Mix

But giving in to the impulse to hunker down in bonds increases the risk that your retirement nest egg may expire before you do. Consider: A study of the longevity of sixty-five-year-old couples by St. Petersburg actuarial firm Moulton & Company found that at least one spouse lived to age eighty-five among 84 percent of the couples, one spouse lived to age ninety in more than 60 percent of the couples, and one made it to age ninety-five in nearly 40 percent of the couples. The upshot: Retirees in their sixties may be looking at another twenty to thirty years of investing, if not more, and even people in their seventies and eighties may have another ten to twenty years ahead of them.

Given those investing time frames, bonds alone won't keep the purchasing power of your portfolio ahead of inflation. You still need stocks to do that. So what stocks-bonds mix is right? That depends on your age, risk tolerance, and other factors. If you've got a very large portfolio, or if income from pensions and Social Security covers most of your living expenses, or if you plan on leaving money to heirs rather than spending your last cent just before you check out, you can afford to focus more on stocks. Generally, though, investors in their early sixties should start somewhere close to the 70 percent stocks–30 percent bonds mix of the Aggressive Portfolio, move toward the fifty-fifty mix of the Middle of the Road Portfolio as they near their seventies, and then gravitate to the 30 percent stocks–70 percent bonds Conservative Portfolio in their eighties.

If you find you need more income than your mix is providing, don't automatically snap up more bonds. Instead try adding dividend-paying funds (such as equity-income funds) to your mix or a few stocks that pay regular dividends. That way you'll boost your income but still have a shot at capital growth that can keep your portfolio ahead of inflation.

CHAPTER 8

How to Find Decent Hired Help

• • • • • • • • • • •

Everybody's Trying to Be Your Adviser

Scientists say that light in a vacuum travels at the speed of 186,000 miles per second squared. Pretty damn quick—but not nearly as fast as the scent of money as it moves around the financial community. No kidding. As soon as you have a bit of money to invest or you're thinking of buying stocks or mutual funds or opening up an IRA, one thing you'll notice is that you can find yourself bombarded by pitches from brokers, financial planners, insurance agents, money managers, bank officers, and other putative financial experts. It's as if investable cash throws off powerful pheromones that tell financial advisers a potential client is lurking nearby and some commissions or other fees may be ready for the taking.

But before you even get to the issue of separating the incompetents and the ethically challenged from the sharp-minded and honest pros, you should ask yourself this question: Do I really need a financial adviser?

For most people, I believe the answer is a qualified no. That is, I think most individuals—and especially the bright inquisitive types I'm sure are reading this book—are capable of choosing and monitoring their investments largely on their own. Choosing and keeping track of investments isn't that difficult, and we're likely to be more vigilant and thoughtful in our investing if we personally take responsibility for our decisions rather than abdicating our responsibility to putative experts.

On the other hand, there may be specific situations in which you can use some intelligent feedback. So I believe in what I call the *financial adviser as training wheels* strategy. You plan on eventually taking control of your own financial life, but you're a little tentative getting started. So you want a bit of help until you get the hang of it. In that case, I think it makes perfect sense to consult an adviser who can help you set up an investment portfolio, choose some mutual funds to get you going, maybe even give you an overall financial checkup to make sure you haven't overlooked other key components in your financial and investing strategy, such as making sure you're taking advantage of tax-advantaged savings accounts at work and that you have the proper amount of life and disability insurance.

You might also want to consider going to a financial pro for advice about a matter that involves such a large portion of your wealth that you feel uncomfortable tackling it on your own. For example, if you are switching jobs, you may want help deciding whether to leave the $500,000 in your company's 401(k) plan or roll it over into an individual retirement account. If you go for the rollover, you might want advice on investing that mammoth sum. Similarly, if you've managed to accumuate enough assets in your lifetime that Uncle Sam's (choose one or more: blimpish, punitive, confiscatory, grossly unfair) estate tax rates will ream the value of the estate you're able to pass on to your heirs, you'll probably want to talk to someone who knows his or her way around the arcane details of estate taxes, wills, and trusts.

But I recommend that you think of your relationship with

financial advisers as a dating relationship, not a marriage. You should be looking to get the advice or services you need and then move on without getting sucked into a long-term relationship. Why? For one thing, it can get expensive. Whether an adviser charges a flat fee, an hourly fee, a percentage of the assets he manages for you, or a commission on each specific investment he sells you, that money adds up. If one way or another you end up paying 1 percent to 2 percent of the value of your investment portfolio to an adviser—and that amount isn't uncommon for ongoing advice and monitoring of your investments—you're giving away a sizable chunk of your returns.

So if you find yourself in a situation where you feel you do need advice from an investing expert, whom should you turn to? A financial planner? A broker? A money manager? Your insurance agent? With few exceptions I consider a financial planner the best place to start, although even there you've got to do some homework to make sure you wind up with someone honest and competent. For reasons I'll point out in a bit, I am much more wary of relying on brokers and insurance agents (even those who claim they're financial planners or essentially do the same job as a financial planner) for help with my overall investing strategy or even for recommendations about specific investments.

WHAT TO LOOK FOR IN A FINANCIAL PLANNER

A good financial planner can work with you in setting an overall strategy that will help you reach your financial goals—and help you choose the investments you need to make that strategy work. If you are looking for advice not just about investing, but also about your overall financial picture, then the planner can create a blueprint known as a *financial plan,* which evaluates all aspects of your financial life from investments to retirement and estate planning.

If you want only investment advice, however, a planner should be able to narrow his focus. Most planners can help you divvy up your investment portfolio among stocks, bonds, and cash, given the goals you want to achieve and your tolerance for risk. Most can also recommend specific mutual funds that are consistent with your asset allocation, and a growing number can recommend no-load funds that are sold through no-transaction-fee networks like Schwab's OneSource mutual fund supermarket.

The difficulty, though, is separating the good planners who can do all these things from the legions of advisers out there who can't. There're no legally binding criteria for using the term *financial planner.* Anyone can hang out a shingle and call himself or herself a financial planner. If someone offers financial advice for a fee, then that person is required to register with either the Securities and Exchange Commission or state securities regulators. (In some cases, planners may register with both.) But the mere act of registering doesn't amount to all that much. There are no professional standards for registering or competency tests one has to meet.

What's more, if someone sells stocks or bonds or mutual funds and is paid solely by commissions those investments generate—as opposed to charging fees for advice—then that person does not have to register as a financial adviser (although the person does have to hold a broker's license if he's selling stocks, mutual funds, or other securities, or an insurance agent's license if he's selling insurance products). That means that brokers who do nothing other than sell load mutual funds or insurance agents whose idea of financial planning is selling life insurance can call themselves financial planners, even though what they do is as far from true financial planning as whiffle ball is to major league baseball.

So if you've decided to hire a financial planner, how do you know you're getting the real thing and not an impostor? Following are ten questions that can help you not only identify true financial planners, but also pick a planner who's right for you.

TEN QUESTIONS TO ASK BEFORE HIRING A FINANCIAL PLANNER

If a planner balks at answering any of these questions or seems evasive, cross that person off your list and move on to the next candidate.

1. ARE YOU REGISTERED WITH THE SEC AND/OR YOUR STATE SECURITIES DEPARTMENT? Anyone who is actually practicing financial planning (as opposed to merely selling stocks or mutual funds or other investments for a commission) should be registered. If the planner's firm manages assets of $25 million or more, the planner is required to be registered with the Securities and Exchange Commission. Otherwise the firm registers with the state securities regulators. In some cases planners may register with both. Either way, registering doesn't guarantee that a planner is competent or honest. However, it at least shows that the planner is aware of the laws governing his or her profession and is abiding by those laws.

2. WHAT PROFESSIONAL CREDENTIALS DO YOU HAVE—AND HOW MANY YEARS' EXPERIENCE WORKING WITH CLIENTS? To make sure you're not just dealing with some bozo who thinks he's pretty good at picking hot stocks or mutual funds, you should restrict yourself to advisers who hold one or more professional designations. For example, about thirty thousand planners nationwide have met the educational requirements and passed the tests that qualify them to be called a certified financial planner (CFP), while another thirty thousand or so advisers have met similar requirements allowing them to call themselves a chartered financial consultant (ChFC). These labels can't assure you that an adviser is competent and has integrity, but at least they tell you an adviser has had training in areas such as investing, taxes, and estate planning and had to pass certain tests to gain the designation. (For a look at what someone has to do to earn these and other titles, see "Deciphering the Alphabet Soup of Credentials" on page 194.)

As for job experience, there's no magic number of years that bestows credibility. That said, I don't particularly want to be the guinea pig for a new planner. I would feel most comfortable with someone who has at least five years of experience dealing with clients.

3. WHAT TYPE OF FINANCIAL PLANNING SERVICES DO YOU MOST OFTEN PROVIDE—AND WHAT KINDS OF INVESTMENTS DO YOU TYPICALLY RECOMMEND? Try to match your needs with a planner's expertise. One way to do that is to also ask the planner to list all the types of investments he or she sells—and to list them roughly in the order in which he or she sells most often. That can give you a clue as to whether someone truly does comprehensive planning or whether the planning title is a guise for pushing certain products.

4. HOW WILL I PAY YOU—AND WILL YOU DISCLOSE TO ME UP FRONT IN WRITING ALL THE FEES AND COMMISSIONS YOU EARN FROM DOING BUSINESS WITH ME? For the most part, planners fall into one of three categories when it comes to compensation:

Fee only: These planners—a distinct minority of about four thousand or so souls—get paid solely for the advice they offer. They accept no commissions on products such as mutual funds or insurance policies. Although their rates vary widely depending on how complex your finances are, you should probably expect to pay in the neighborhood of $2,000 to $5,000 for a comprehensive financial plan from a fee-only planner. If you're looking for something simpler, such as help in putting together a mutual fund portfolio, you can probably get by for a flat fee of half or less than half of that amount, or you may be able to hire the planner at a rate of $80 to $400 an hour.

Generally, I believe this is the ideal compensation arrangement for planners because it eliminates the built-in conflict of interest that commissioned salespeople operate under. If you're investing a small sum of money, though, paying $80 bucks an hour or a $2,000 flat fee would be impractical, so you might have to opt for a planner compensated one of the other two ways mentioned here. For a referral to a fee-only planner near you, call the National Association of Personal Financial Advisors (888-FEE-ONLY), an organization that has trademarked the term *fee only* and whose membership consists solely of fee-only planners.

Commission only: These planners make their living exclusively from the commissions on the products they sell. Those commissions can range from a modest 3 percent or so on some load mutual funds to a more sizable 5 percent or more on some funds. Annuities, on the other hand, can easily generate commissions of 4 percent to as high as 10 percent in some cases, while the take on insurance policies can be even higher—50 percent to 100 percent of the first year's premium. Whenever you're dealing with someone depending on commissions, there's always an inherent conflict between your interests and the adviser's. So make sure you take that into account when you review the planner's recommendations.

Fee and commission: These planners, also known as *fee-based advisers,* earn a combination of fees and commissions. Typically they charge a fee for the financial plan they draw up for you—say, $1,000—and then you get credit for the first $1,000 of commissions on the investments you buy through the planner. If you drum up more in commissions, then your bill goes up. Alternatively, if you don't require a plan but are looking primarily for help with specific invesments, the planner will simply recommend ones that carry a commission, much the same as a commission-only planner would. This arrangement is the most popular of the three compensation methods. It allows planners to say they're not tied exclusively to commissions (which carry the dread specter of conflict of interest) yet at the same time gives them the flexibility to charge commissions if they have to.

5. BESIDES THE FEES AND COMMISSIONS I PAY, DO YOU EARN MONEY FROM ME IN ANY OTHER WAY?

Some planners have other business relationships that could influence their recommendations and even (God forbid!) cause them to put their interests ahead of yours. For example, a planner could receive free trips or other incentives from an investment firm or insurance company for selling annuities, mutual funds, or other products. Similarly, a planner could receive referral fees or otherwise benefit from referring you to certain insurance agents, accountants, or attorneys.

6. HAVE YOU EVER HAD ANY RUN-INS WITH FEDERAL OR STATE REGULATORS—EVEN MINOR ONES—OR EVER HAD A CLIENT FILE AN ARBITRATION CLAIM OR OTHER LEGAL PROCEEDINGS AGAINST YOU?

If the answer is yes, ask for details. Depending on how serious the infractions were, you may want to just move on to another planner. Of course, a dishonest planner isn't likely to spill the beans on himself. So you should also check independently with federal and state regulators at the phone numbers I give at the end of the chapter.

7. WILL YOU GIVE ME A COPY OF YOUR ADV— PARTS I *AND* II? Planners are required to provide you with part II of the ADV form they file with the SEC or state regulators. (ADV stands for adviser.) That section of the ADV includes information about a planner's job experience and credentials, investment strategies, any potential conflicts of interest, and how the planner is compensated. In part I of the ADV, a planner must disclose whether he's ever run afoul of the SEC or other regulators. Planners aren't required to give you this part of the form, but, hey, why not ask for it—and if the planner says something like "Na na na *na* na, we don't have to give you part I" or makes up some bogus excuse about why he can't provide it ("My dog ate my file cabinet"), then you can move on to another planner.

8. COULD YOU GIVE ME THE NAMES OF THREE CLIENTS YOU'VE HAD FOR AT LEAST THREE YEARS? Yes, in some ways talking to the people the planner himself refers you to is a ridiculous exercise. I mean, is he going to set you up with disgruntled clients? On the other hand, you can probably get a sense of how the planner works with clients, how responsive he is to questions, how accessible he is, and whether or not you would simply like his style.

9. CAN I SEE COPIES OF THREE FINANCIAL PLANS YOU'VE DONE FOR CLIENTS, ONE WHOSE FINANCES ARE SIMILAR TO MINE AND TWO WHOSE AREN'T? Looking over some of the strategies a planner has prepared should give you a good idea of the types of recommendations he's made in the past and how detailed the advice is. And by perusing the plans of three clients in different financial circumstances, you can get an idea of how much each plan is tailored to individual clients' needs.

10. HOW CAN BOTH OF US EVALUATE HOW GOOD A JOB YOU'VE DONE? The real test of how good a job a planner has done is how well the advice holds up after you leave the office. That can be difficult to gauge. Let's say the stock or fund portfolio the planner assembled sinks 20 percent within a year. If the market overall is thriving, then the planner's got some explaining to do. But if the market overall has also dropped by a similar amount, then pointing fingers at the planner is useless. You and the planner should agree on some benchmarks for monitoring the planner's work. You should also talk about how often you want to do that and how much it will cost. Just make sure that the planner doesn't use occasional monitoring as an invitation to make constant changes to your portfolio—and to charge ever more fees.

DECIPHERING THE ALPHABET SOUP OF CREDENTIALS

Take a look at the business card of a financial planner or other adviser and you're likely to see a long string of letters after the name: CFP, ChFC, CFS, ETC. Here's a quick explanation of the most common designations, along with my own highly subjective judgment about which ones you should value most when looking for a planner or adviser:

CFP: The certified financial planner designation is the one that, in my opinion, carries the most credibility in the financial planning field. To qualify for the CFP, an adviser must have completed financial planning courses in areas ranging from investing to estate planning and passed a ten-hour, two-day exam covering a variety of financial planning topics. The adviser must also have a bachelor's degree and three years of financial planning work experience (or five years of experience without the degree) and must participate in continuing education courses. For the names of CFPs in your area, contact the Institute of Certified Financial Planners in Denver (800-282-PLAN; www.icfp.org) or the International Association for Financial Planning in Atlanta (888-806-PLAN; www.iafp.org).

ChFC: The chartered financial consultant designation is bestowed by the American College in Bryn Mawr, Pennsylvania, to advisers who complete a ten-course financial planning curriculum, pass a two-hour exam for each of the ten courses, and have one to three years of business experience, which makes the ChFC at least comparable to the CFP in terms of academic rigor. My main hesitation in choosing an adviser with a ChFC, however, is that historically this designation has gone primarily to life insurance agents looking to broaden their practice. So if you deal with a ChFC, just make sure you're not being pitched life insurance products under the guise of financial planning. The American Society of CLU & ChFC in Bryn Mawr, Pennsylvania (888-ChFC-CLU; www.agents-online.com/ASCLU/index.html), can provide the names of advisers with the ChFC designation in your area.

PFS: The personal financial specialist designation goes to certified public accountants who have passed a six-hour exam covering six financial planning topics and who have 250 hours of financial planning experience in each of the three years prior to receiving the designation. Only about 2,500 CPAs have the PFS designation, and they tend to cater to a more affluent clientele. So for most people the CFP is the more logical choice. But if you insist on dealing with a PFS, contact the American Institute of Certified Public Accountants in New York City (888-999-9256; www.aicpa.org).

MBA: You see the master's of business administration popping up on the cards of lots of financial planners, brokers, and money managers these days. My reaction: Big deal, it's just not very relevant to providing personal financial advice. If, on the other hand, you are looking for someone to help you launch a hostile takeover attempt on a Fortune 500 company using zero-coupon junk bonds for financing, well, then maybe a suspender-wearing MBA is just the person you need.

CFS: This designation—the certified fund specialist—is granted by the Institute of Business and Finance in La Jolla, California, to people who complete a sixty-hour course of studies about funds and pass a final exam. How impressed should you be if you see this on a business card? Not very, in my opinion. I see the CFS as an example of how credentials are becoming marketing tools as much as manifestations of true financial expertise. I mean, are mutual funds really complicated and specialized enough to require their own professional designation? What's next—a master's degree in certificates of deposit? I wouldn't go so far as to say that a CFS is a bald-faced attempt by some advisers to "buy" credibility. But seeing it on an adviser's business card wouldn't make me any more likely to hire him.

A BROKER BY ANY OTHER NAME . . . IS STILL A BROKER

It seems as if brokers are doing everything they can these days to avoid using the term *broker*. They call themselves account executives, financial advisers, investment consultants . . . anything, apparently, but brokers. One brokerage firm even tries to pass off its brokers with the grandiose (and completely made-up) title of personal CFOs (chief financial officers). Part of the reason for this chameleonlike effort to adopt a new identity is that many people have bad associations with the term *broker*.

For example, a 1997 poll by the brokerage industry's own trade group, the Securities Industry Association (SIA), found that 70 percent of those surveyed agreed with the statement, "Brokers are more concerned about earning commissions on products they sell than they are about providing clients with good investment advice."

In recent years the brokerage industry has made a big push to become, or at least appear, more advice oriented than sales oriented. Most major brokerage firms as well as regional outfits offer some type of financial planning service, typically a financial plan that's computer generated for free or for a relatively modest fee.

But even though brokerage firms would have you believe that they are a bastion of savvy securities research and a valuable source of comprehensive financial advice, in my opinion they remain essentially sales operations at their core. And in the final analysis the main job for the bulk of the country's 562,000 or so licensed brokers is to push products for commissions or to get you to sign up for fee-based programs that transfer anywhere from 1 percent to 2 percent of the assets in your account into the brokerage firm's pocket (and from there into the broker's) each year.

Why do I say this? Well, let's just take a look at how brokerage firms actually make their money. In 1996, according to figures published by the SIA, New York Stock Exchange (NYSE) firms had total revenues of just over $120 billion. And how much of that came from securities the firms held for investment? A little over $1 billion. Commissions, on the other hand, totaled just over $18 billion. In other words, NYSE brokerage firms took in about eighteen times as much money in *sales commissions* as they earned by investing their money. The biggest chunk of revenues was in a category with the catchy title "Other Securities Related," which includes fees for consulting on mergers and acquisitions, doing private placement of securities, that sort of thing. But what I believe these figures show is that brokerage firms don't make money so much by investing as they do by telling you what to invest in and charging you a fee or commission for doing so.

So in my highly subjective opinion, a broker generally isn't a good place to start if you want comprehensive and unbiased financial advice. Even in the cases where the firm or the broker may be able to provide you with a decent financial plan, it's what happens afterward that I worry about. I think there's too big a temptation to load you up with products that generate high commissions—and then to do it again and again.

If you do decide to work with a broker, you should pretty much put him through the ten questions I suggested earlier for financial planners, with a few modifications. For example, unless the broker is registered as an investment adviser (most aren't), he or she won't be able to provide you with the ADV forms I mentioned.

If you are doing anything more than putting a small amount of money in a few mutual funds, however, you should definitely check whether the broker has a record of being disciplined by the SEC, state securities regulators, or the self-regulatory group that oversees brokers, the National Association of Securities Dealers (NASD). You can do that by tapping into the Central Registration Depository, which contains such information as the broker's education, work experience, and disciplinary history, if any. You can get the info for a broker by calling the NASD's public disclosure number (800-280-9999) or by contacting securities regulators. You can get the number for the regulator in your state by calling your state government's central number or by checking out the Web site of the North American Securities Administrators Association (www.nasaa.org/regulator/index.html).

LIES, DAMNED LIES, AND BROKER'S PITCHES

Brokers are probably at their most creative in coming up not with terrific investment ideas, but with lines to convince you to invest money with them. Following are ten common ploys they will use to lure you in. In many cases these pitches appear in telephone cold calls—that is, unsolicited calls many brokers make to people they don't even know. Brokers refer to this type of heavy-duty phone prospecting, during which they may call hundreds of potential ~~suckers~~ clients in the course of a day, as *smile and dial*. But sometimes even a broker you know may resort to these or similar lines to get you to invest. It's always possible, of course, that a broker you barely know or don't know at all is calling to let you in on the investment opportunity of a lifetime. And it's also possible that tomorrow you'll find a cashier's check for $1 million in your mailbox sent to you by a wealthy cousin seventeen times removed whom you didn't even know existed. My advice: Never commit to an investment purely on the basis of a phone call.

THE PITCH	THE REALITY
1. With my firm's contacts on Wall Street, I can give you an inside track on the stock market.	What you're getting the inside track to is the inventory of stocks or mutual funds or other "packaged products" that the firm is pushing that particular day.
2. Don't get hung up on sales commissions. What really matters is how much an investment earns for you, not what you pay me to get it.	The more you pay in commissions, the more an investment has to earn for you to make a profit. Although brokers are loath to admit it, fees and commissions act as a major drag on your investments.
3. The way to make money is by reacting quickly to market conditions. I'll help you keep on top of the market.	He's got part of this right: The way for the *broker* to make money is by having you buy and sell stocks in a vain attempt to outsmart the market.
4. We're only letting our best clients in on this deal.	Yeah, and this guy probably only sends Christmas cards to his few hundred "closest" friends. If there are any special deals to be had, you can be sure they're going to big institutional investors or clients who have six figures or more invested with the firm.

THE PITCH	THE REALITY
5. You can't go wrong with tax-advantaged investments.	Really? So why did investors lose billions of dollars in tax-sheltered limited partnerships in the 1980s?
6. I can't guarantee I'll be able to get you in on this great investment if you don't act right now.	Translation: The end of the month is coming up, and I haven't made my commission quota, so I've got to sell some stuff fast.
7. This investment is such a sure thing, I've even put my mom into it.	The sad thing is that he probably did put his mom into the investment—not to mention his dad, best friend, a dozen high school acquaintances, and 10 out of the last 150 people he called. Let's hope Mom doesn't make out too badly.
8. This company has a shot at being tomorrow's_____ (fill in one: Microsoft, Intel, Coca-Cola).	One question: How many clients did this guy put into Microsoft or Intel *before* people realized these companies would dominate their industries?
9. I come across more investing ideas in one day than you'll hear in a year. Let me put the benefit of my insider's knowledge to work for you.	Brokers do come across tons of investing ideas every day. Problem is, many brokers spend more time *selling* as many of them as they can rather than doing rigorous analysis to weed out the superior ones from the mediocre or downright bad.
10. Invest now, and you'll be getting in with the smart money.	By the time a broker is calling a small investor like you, the smart money not only has already gotten in—it's looking to get out by selling to you.

THE LOWDOWN ON OTHER TYPES OF HIRED HELP

In sheer numbers, brokers and financial planners are the people you're most likely to run across when you're looking for someone to help you with your investing. But they're hardly the only ones out there clamoring for your business. Here's a quick rundown on a few other types of financial advisers you may run across or who may come looking for you:

INSURANCE AGENTS. You've heard the expression "To a man with a hammer, everything looks like a nail"? Well, that's the first idea that comes to mind whenever I hear the words *insurance agent*. As sales of life insurance policies have been rather stagnant in recent years, the nation's 220,000 or so life insurance agents are looking more and more to portray themselves as broad-based financial advisers. Problem is, in too many cases their knee-jerk reaction to solving any financial problem is selling some form of insurance: "Looking for a way to save for your child's education? How about a tax-deferred variable annuity? Want to accumulate a retirement nest egg? Our universal life policies provide great returns and even offer a shot at tax-free gains. Interested in a safe way to get high tax-deferred yields? Our fixed annuities come with high payouts and assure you'll never lose any of your principal."

While life insurance clearly should play a major role in your overall financial plan as a way to protect you against medical costs that could deplete your resources or to replace income if you die, these days insurance agents increasingly look for ways to peddle life insurance as investments. And frankly, I don't believe insurance makes a very good investment. The fees are usually too high, the returns too low, the products far too complicated, the disclosure not even close to being adequate for anyone to evaluate the products . . . are you getting the impression that I'm not very high on going to an insurance agent for financial advice?

There are, as always, exceptions. If an agent also happens to be a certified financial planner—that is, someone who actually holds the CFP or ChFC designation, not just an agent who calls himself a financial planner—then I might consider working with that person. But even then I think you have to be wary about being steered toward investments that have an insurance component, such as fixed or variable annuities or variable life insurance policies.

MONEY MANAGERS. In popular parlance, this term is often used rather loosely to mean anyone who helps people deal with financial issues. But in financial circles, a money manager is someone who puts together a portfolio of stocks, bonds, or a combination of the two for clients. Historically, those clients have tended to be ones with big bucks to invest: a mutual fund, a pension fund, or a wealthy individual with upward of $1 million of assets. But in recent years Wall Street brokerage firms and others have begun peddling money managers to middle-class clients who may have as little as $50,000 or so to invest. The firms claim that hiring your own private money manager beats investing in a mutual fund because you get a customized portfolio and more individual attention.

In my experience, these claims are usually specious. The brokerage programs often result in some money managers overseeing thousands of accounts, which means that most of them wind up with a strikingly similar mix of securities—not much different from a mutual fund. But the fees are generally much higher than you would pay in funds. One of the most popular forms of money manager accounts peddled today—so-called wrap accounts—often charge individuals 2 percent to 3 percent of assets each year, a drain on earnings that virtually guarantees returns will seriously lag those of the overall market.

CPAs. Although I have the highest regard for the financial acumen of CPAs, I don't think their training necessarily makes them great candidates for dispensing personal financial advice. So I would be much more likely to opt for a traditional financial planner than a CPA, unless the CPA had the PFS designation, could claim several years' experience not just in accounting but in financial planning, and was clearly willing to make specific recommendations.

INVESTMENT CONSULTANTS. This term (as well as its cousin, *financial consultant*) is vague and essentially meaningless but often used by brokers or other people to give the impression that they do something a lot more grand than simply sell invest-ment products for a commission. Similarly, it could be the title of a person at a bank or S&L or other financial institution who peddles securities or other financial products. In any case, it is not a term regulated by any government agency or that requires someone to demonstrate financial proficiency of any kind. So if this term is the best that someone can come up with to tout his expertise, I would be wary of doing business with that person and at the very least would look long and hard into that person's credentials and qualifications.

WHERE TO COMPLAIN IF YOU THINK YOU'VE BEEN FLEECED

Despite our best efforts to steer clear of frauds, cheats, and incompetents, we sometimes end up in the clutches of someone who bilks us or puts us into inappropriate or losing investments. So what should you do if you find yourself in that position? Well, the first thing is to complain loudly to self-regulatory organizations, professional associations, and state and federal regulators. You may also have to complain often; it can sometimes take months or longer before you get any feedback, let alone results. But if you don't start there and document your complaint, your chances of getting any kind of resolution of your problem are slim.

Following is a list of several regulatory agencies and professional organizations you can complain to about specific types of advisers. In most cases I name more than one agency or organization because it's sometimes difficult to determine which regulator oversees the adviser you've been dealing with. It's even possible that more than one regulator may have jurisdiction. So I suggest you start with the scattergun approach and contact all regulators and trade associations that might oversee your adviser. As you get more information about which office has specific jurisdiction—or seems most willing to help you—you can refine your efforts. Outline your complaint in writing—and be sure to send a copy to the offending adviser as well; it doesn't hurt to let him or her know you're mad as hell and plan to seek restitution.

If you have a complaint about a . . .	Contact the . . .
Financial planner	• Securities and Exchange Commission Office of Investor Education and Assistance (202-942-8090; www.sec.gov) • State securities agency (get the name and number of your state agency through the North American Securities Administrators Association, 888-84NASAA; www.nasaa.org)

If you have a complaint about a . . .	Contact the . . .
Broker	• National Association of Securities Dealers (800-289-9999; www.nasd.com) • SEC Office of Investor Education and Assistance
Money manager	• Securities and Exchange Commission Office of Investor Education and Assistance • State securities agency
Insurance agent	• State insurance department (call directory assistance in your state capital or contact the National Association of Insurance Commissioners, 816-842-3600; www.naic.org) • SEC and/or state securities agency (if the agent presents himself as a financial planner and/or sells variable annuities, mutual funds, or other investments)
CPA	• Securities and Exchange Commission Office of Investor Education and Assistance (if the CPA is acting as a financial planner) • State securities agency (if the CPA is acting as a financial planner) • State Board of Accountancy (you can get the number for the board in your state through the National Association of State Boards of Accountancy, 615-880-4200; www.nasba.org)

CHAPTER 9

Reliable Sources: Where to Find Investing Info You Can Trust

• • • • • • • • • • •

Develop a Sense of Detachment

L isten to the financial press touting the benefits of the plethora of information available to investors today and you come away with the impression that unless you're out there flipping through cable stations, gleaning nuggets of advice from the talking heads, speed-reading every investment publication you can get your hands on for the best stocks or funds, surfing your way through thousands of investing Web sites, or staying in constant touch with your broker via cell phone or beeper, you're a dinosaur doomed to subpar returns and, eventually, financial extinction as more nimble investors scoop up the best investments, leaving you with the dross.

But I'm convinced that in many cases the sheer volume of information and advice hurts investors because it paralyzes them with indecision or leads them to *act* on every bit of information or advice that comes their way. So let me be clear about why I've included this chapter in the book. While I think it's generally a mistake to invest on the basis of the lastest news or bits of information you glean from TV, publications, the Internet, and other sources, I believe there's an inherent value to being an informed investor who is aware of what's going on in the investment world. I also think it's a good idea to keep track of your own investments, not necessarily on a daily, weekly, or even monthly basis. But occasionally—say, every quarter or so—you should check in just to make sure nothing has gone drastically wrong.

What's the benefit of such monitoring if you're not going to translate it into action? Well, if you're keeping tabs on the goings-on in the financial world, you're more likely to get a sense of the ebb and flow of different investments, a sense that there will be runups in the stock market that are followed by occasional (and inevitable) pullbacks in stock prices. You will develop a sense of context, of how the financial world works, and, most of all, of the realization that ups and downs are a part of the natural order of the financial markets. Market setbacks and turmoil aren't things you've got to whip yourself into a frenzy about or times of crisis when you've got to scrap your investment strategy and start over because the world has changed.

So when you're being bombarded with statistics, data, advice, and outright blather from all forms of media, I believe it's crucial that *you maintain a sense of detachment from it all.* Of course, that's just the opposite of what the financial press wants you to feel. They want you to feel that only by reading their articles, listening to their show, or surfing their Web sites can you weather whatever "crisis" is at hand. Fact is, they could be a help if they clearly warned us of crises in advance, but that's not possible since no one can foretell the future. So instead they try to make it sound as if they're going to give us a useful way to react to what's already happened. Too late. Any action you take after the fact isn't likely to do much good anyway. So when you're watching a news anchor telling you about how the U.S. market is falling apart, the Hong Kong market is in a tailspin, and the *world stock markets are in crisis* . . . try to think of it as if it were a curious spectacle going on on another planet that really doesn't affect you very much. Listen in, be aware of what's going on, try to absorb any lessons that you might apply in the future—but don't go making big changes in your portfolio.

With that sense of detachment in mind, the rest of this chapter will detail places, starting with the newspaper, where you can find information to help you monitor the investments you have and to get information that might help you evaluate the ones you own or choose new ones.

DECIPHERING THE NEWSPAPER'S STOCK TABLES

The financial sections of daily newspapers in most cities of any size do a pretty decent job of helping you stay abreast of the major business and economic stories of the day. A quick read and you should have no trouble keeping up with what companies and stocks are in the news, whether interest rates are going up and down, whether the economy is cruising along nicely or headed for recession, the outlook for inflation—all the sorts of things you need to know to remain informed about the business and investing scene.

CAN YOU PASS THIS STOCK SYMBOL QUIZ?

To avoid confusion when companies have similar names, brokers refer to stocks by their ticker symbols—typically one to four capital letters—when placing orders. Following are three real stock ticker symbols along with names of actual and fictitious firms. Can you match the three symbols below to the real company that uses it?

1. PIN
   a. National Needle Co.
   b. Wrestling Federation of America
   c. AMF Bowling Corp.
2. NUT
   a. Psychiatric Centers of America
   b. Mauna Loa Macadamia Partners
   c. Screw and Bolt, Inc.
3. POT
   a. Kitchenware, Inc.
   b. Marijuana Growers, Ltd.
   c. Potash Corp. of Saskatchewan

Answers: 1, c; 2, b; 3, c (You were thinking b?)

But people who aren't regular readers of the business section—or those who breeze through it but don't look very closely—could find themselves a bit stymied by the financial section's long tables of tiny type, weird abbreviations, and unusual signs. Yes, the stock listings. Like most information dealing with the financial world, these listings seemed designed to confuse, to obfuscate, to make it more difficult than necessary to find out what's going on. In fact, though, once you learn to decipher the arcane code they're written in, you'll find that these tables are a quick and convenient way to check up on the prices of any stocks you own. In this section, I've reproduced a small portion of the stock tables from *The Wall Street Journal* from early May 1998. Going from left to right, let's take a quick run through the listing for Coca-Cola.

52 Weeks					Yld		Vol				Net
Hi	Lo	Stock	Sym	Div	%	PE	100s	Hi	Lo	Close	Chg
25	10¾	Coastcast	PAR		. . .	15	688	22¹¹⁄₁₆	22⅛	22⁵⁄₁₆	-¹⁄₁₆
81⅜	51¹⁵⁄₁₆	CocaCola	KO	.60	.8	47	23571	76⅝	75⅝	76	-¹⁄₁₆
s20¹⁵⁄₁₆	11⅞	CCFemsa ADR	KOF		. . .	. . .	5727	18¼	16¾	17⅝	+⁹⁄₁₆
s41⁷⁄₁₆	18⅞	CocaColaEnt	CCE	.16f	.4	94	4781	38⅛	37⅜	37⅝	+⅛
16¾	7¹⁄₁₆	Coeur dAMn	CDE	.15	1.4	dd	1045	11¹⁄₁₆	10¹¹⁄₁₆	10⅞	-¼
18¹⁵⁄₁₆	11¹¹⁄₁₆	Coeur dAMn pf		1.49	10.4	. . .	132	14⅜	14³⁄₁₆	14⁵⁄₁₆	. . .
58¾	32½	Cognizant	CZT	.12	.2	27	1524	52⅛	51½	51⁹⁄₁₆	-⁹⁄₁₆

52-week Hi Lo: This shows you the highest and the lowest price at which Coke's stock has traded over the past fifty-two weeks. This stat really doesn't tell you very much, other than the fact that the stock's had a pretty impressive runup over the past year, increasing 59 percent from a low of $51¹⁵⁄₁₆ to a high of $81⅜. That doesn't mean Coke's stock is likely to continue to rise at that rate or, for that matter, that it's likely to stagnate or fall after such a quick climb.

Stock: The name of the stock. With Coca-Cola, the name of the company issuing the stock is pretty self-evident. But some of the abbreviations could flummox a master code cracker. Below Coke, for example, is the name "Coeur dAMn," which refers to

Coeur d'Alene Mines, an Idaho company with interests in gold and silver mines in Nevada, Chile, and New Zealand.

Sym: This is the trading symbol for the stock, which is the one-to-four-letter code that traders use when buying or selling the stock or when they check its price on computerized quote systems. Whenever you're buying or selling a stock, you should always use this symbol to be sure you're identifying the right stock. For example, if you told a broker you wanted to buy shares of Coca-Cola but didn't mention the symbol KO, the broker could mistakenly buy shares of Coca-Cola Enterprises, a bottler and distributor of Coke and other beverages that is listed below Coke with the symbol CCE. Practically the only interesting thing about these symbols is that sometimes they're funny or clever little plays on the name of the company. For example, MALT stands for the Lion Brewery, SLOT is for Colorado casino operator Anchor Gaming Co., and SEW is the symbol for the Singer sewing machine company.

Div: The stock's annual dividend, if any, based on the most recent dividend paid. (Most companies pay dividends quarterly, although some may pay dividends semiannually, annually, or, rarely, monthly.) In some cases a small "x" may appear next to the dividend, indicating that the stock is "ex-dividend." That means that the latest dividend payment will go to investors who owned the stock before it went ex-dividend, not to ones who buy it after the "x" appears. Investors who buy the stock after the ex-dividend date aren't being cheated, though, since the stock's price automatically adjusts to account for the fact that a new investor will miss that dividend payment.

Yld %: The annual dividend as a percentage of the stock price. At a sixty-cent annual dividend per share, Coke's stock has a modest yield of 0.8 percent. The yield figure changes each day as the stock price goes up and down.

PE: This is the stock's price-earnings ratio based on the closing market price and the most recent four quarters' earnings. In the case of Coke, the PE ratio is 47, or about 1½ times the market PE ratio at that time. In some cases a stock's PE might not be meaningful. For example, if a company had an unusually bad year in which it earned only $.10 a share but was expected to earn its usual $2 or so a share in the coming year, its stock could sell at, say, $30 a share, which would put its PE at 300 ($30 divided by $.10). In cases where the PE ratio is greater than 100, the *Journal* puts a "cc" in that column. When there is a "dd" listed in the PE column (as is the case for Coeur dAMn, which is listed just below Coca-Cola Enterprises), that indicates the company had a loss. If there are no earnings, it's impossible to calculate a price-earnings ratio.

Vol 100s: The trading volume in hundreds. Add two zeros to the 23,571 figure listed in this column for Coke, and you now know that 2,357,100 shares of Coke traded on the New York Stock Exchange that day. The breed of investors known as *technical analysts* often plot daily trading volumes, comparing them with moving averages of the prices of those stocks. They believe that at times the relationship between volume and prices can provide key buy or sell signals. And I say you've got about an equal chance of finding key buy and sell signals by charting Alan Greenspan's horoscope.

Hi Lo: These figures show the high and the low price for the stock for that day. I can't think of a reason in the world this should be of interest to anyone.

Close: The stock's closing price for the day. So now you know what your stock is worth as of 4 P.M. the previous day.

Net Chg: The difference between the stock's closing price at the end of the day and the previous quoted closing price. In this case, Coca-Cola shares were worth ⅟₁₆ of a dollar (6.25 cents) less at the end of the day than they had been at the end of the previous day. I can't imagine a case where I would ever buy or sell a stock on the basis of one day's activity in the stock market or, for that matter, even that of several days.

MANY NEWSPAPERS' FUND TABLES STINK (BUT THEY'RE IMPROVING)

While some newspapers provide only the name of the fund, the net asset value, and the change in net asset value from the previous day, more and more seem to be improving their fund listings to provide real information. Following is a sample of one of the better fund tables—the one from the Sunday *New York Times*—along with an explanation of what the various figures and notations mean.

One quick note: I don't believe you have to keep track of your funds' performance every week. In fact, to the extent that checking in often might lead to the temptation to shift your fund holdings, frequent monitoring of your funds can be detrimental to your financial health. Certainly once a month is more than enough to be checking in on your funds' performance, and if you want to let it go to once a quarter, that's fine, too.

Fund Family Fund Name	Type	Rating	NAV	Wkly. % Ret.	YTD % Ret.	1-Yr. % Ret.	3-Yr. % Ret.
T Rowe Price	(800) 638-5660						
Balanced	DH	3/4	17.90	- 0.2	+ 9.0	+21.0	+18.7
BlChpGro	LB	5/5	27.58	- 0.4	+14.1	+32.9	+30.4
CATaxFBd	SL	4/3	10.76	+ 0.4	+ 1.0	+ 8.6	+ 7.4
CapApprec	DH	3/4	15.59	- 1.0	+ 6.0	+17.3	+16.9
CapOpp	MG	2/4	18.81	- 0.6	+13.2	+36.2	+23.9
CorpInc	CL	NA	10.37	- 0.2	+ 2.5	+13.8	NA
DivGrow	LB	5/5	21.72	- 0.5	+ 9.1	+30.0	+28.6
DivSmCap d	SG	NA	11.58	- 1.9	+ 8.2	NA	NA
EmMktBd	IB	5/5	13.60	- 0.8	+ 4.2	+12.3	+25.0
EmMktStk d	EM	2/4	11.56	- 3.5	- 1.0	- 6.7	+ 2.7

1. Fund Family: Each listing begins with the name of the mutual fund company, in this case T. Rowe Price, and that fund family's toll-free phone number, which you can call with questions about a fund.

2. Fund name: Immediately below the fund family, the company's funds are listed by name alphabetically.

3. Type: This is the category that fund-rating firm Morningstar has assigned the fund. T. Rowe Price Balanced has a "DH" designation, which stands for "domestic hybrid," a type of fund that typically invests in a mix of stocks and bonds. Immediately below is the listing for T. Rowe Price Blue Chip Growth, which is in the "LB," or "large blend," category, which means it invests in a blend of both large growth stocks and large value stocks. *The New York Times* gives a brief explanation of what these categories mean. But unless you're familiar with the Morningstar classification system, those explanations aren't likely to mean a whole lot to you. For more information on the categories, check out the Morningstar Mutual Funds publications mentioned later in this chapter.

4. Rating: This is another feature I like about the *Times'* listings. Notice that there are two numbers separated by a slash following a fund's name—3/4 in the case of T. Rowe Price Balanced. The first number shows how a fund ranked on a scale of 1 to 5 (5 is the highest rating, 1 the lowest) over the past three years versus one of four broad groups of funds, either all domestic stock funds, international stock funds, taxable bond funds, or tax-exempt bond funds. The second rating compares a fund against a narrower group—that is, funds within its same category, domestic hybrid funds in the case of T. Rowe Price Balanced. These ratings are *risk adjusted,* which means that if two companies had exactly the same returns but one took higher risks to get that return, the lower-risk fund would get a higher rating.

You should focus on the *second* of the two ratings. The first one really tells you more about which kinds of funds are being favored by the trends in today's market. By checking out the second rating, however, you can often get a clue about the manager's ability versus his or her peers. If a manager of a small-company growth fund—one that invests in fast-growing small companies and has the "SG" designation—gets a lousy first rating but a great second rating, it could show that the manager is doing a pretty good job in a difficult situation—namely, a market where small stocks aren't thriving as well as their big counterparts.

While these ratings can provide insights, you shouldn't rely on them exclusively when evaluating funds. If you buy only funds that have the highest first ratings today, you will end up with the types of funds that are favored in today's market. As market trends change, funds can slip from the top of the ratings and ones that are lagging today may surge to the top tomorrow. Even concentrating on funds with high second ratings doesn't guarantee future success, since a manager who is hot now might be employing a strategy that's excelled under market conditions for the past few years but could falter.

5. NAV: The net asset value of a single share of the fund. This number will typically change a bit from day to day but doesn't tell you much. Remember, too, that if the fund makes a distribution—pays a dividend or a capital gain to shareholders—the NAV will go down, even though the change in the NAV attributable to the distribution doesn't affect the value of your account. (You get cash or additional shares to make up for the lower NAV.) As far as being a productive use of your time, I'd say that tracking the NAV of your fund ranks up there with playing computer solitaire.

6. Wkly % Ret.: The percentage gain or loss for your fund over the past week. Ignore it. Memo to the *Times:* Delete this useless number and replace it with something moderately useful, like the fund's annual expenses.

7. 1–Yr. % Ret.: The percentage gain or loss for your fund over the past year.

8. 3–Yr. % Ret.: The annualized percentage gain or loss for your fund over the past three years. Both this number and the one-year return above can give you an idea of how your fund has fared over the past one and three years, but only if you compare the numbers versus those of similar funds. Fortunately the *Times* makes that easy by also running a "Weekly Performance" table that provides the median (and top and bottom quartile) returns for the year to date, the past year, and the past three years for virtually all Morningstar categories of funds.

PERSONAL FINANCE MAGAZINES AND NEWSLETTERS: DO THESE RAGS LEAD TO RICHES?

The most popular personal finance magazines such as *Money*, *Smart Money*, *Kiplinger's*, and *Worth* all do a good job of educating their readers about the fundamentals of investing and keeping readers abreast of the latest developments in the financial markets. And if you're looking for an easy and sometimes entertaining way to learn about investing, stay on top of the latest trends, and even pick up practical tips that might make you some money, I think these magazines offer good value for a few bucks an issue.

But to get the most value out of them, you've got to remember to distinguish your needs as an investor from theirs as a publishing venture. By that I mean that these are monthly magazines, so they're going to come out with new picks, new investments, and new advice twelve times a year, sometimes more if they publish special issues. I don't think most investors need to buy new investments or make adjustments to their portfolio twelve times a year or, for that matter, even half that many times. In my opinion, the frequency of personal finance publications leads to two potential problems. The first is that since a good part of these publications is given over to a new set of stock, fund, and other investment recommendations each month, you might be tempted to fool around with your investments more than you should.

The second potential problem I see is that sometimes the pressure on magazines to say something new that's also useful leads to some pretty awful stories. One publication that I won't embarrass by naming here ran a story about the joys of investing in new mutual funds. To the magazine's credit, it updated the story later, noting that some of the funds it had recommended did okay for a while, then petered out. But instead of chalking this up as an example of why it's just a bad idea in general to try to boost your returns by betting on which new funds might excel, the magazine came to a startlingly different (and, to my mind, dumb) conclusion: The right way to invest in new funds was to buy them and then jump out before performance begins to lag, sort of the way you play hot stocks (an idea I also think is dumb). To my utter astonishment, the magazine then embarked on a story of how to get in and out of hot new funds, a strategy that would lead to punishing taxes and is impossible to pull off on a practical level anyway. I saw this as an example of a publication trying a bit too hard to say something unique, to look a lot smarter than its competitors—and, in my opinion, ultimately doing a disservice to its readers. Fortunately I think this type of story is more an exception than the rule.

As for newsletters, I think most are less helpful to investors than personal finance magazines, even though their annual subscription prices can run as high as a few hundred bucks a year. Few of them offer a coherent view of the investing process or educate their readers about long-term investing strategies. Instead most push the editor's own often highly idiosyncratic take on the markets, usually backed up by reams of charts, graphs, and statistical analysis that often defy human understanding. Many others are little more than tip sheets, the financial equivalent of the pamphlets bettors at the racetrack can buy when they want to know who's favored in the eighth at Belmont. Generally, therefore, I don't believe it's worthwhile for investors to subscribe to these letters.

Given that buildup, you can safely assume I'm not going to rattle off the names of a dozen investment newsletters you might sample. In fact, I'm going to mention only four, which isn't to say there aren't others that might be worthwhile.

FOR FUND INVESTORS

Morningstar Fund Investor ($79 a year, twelve issues, 800-735-0700): If you really want to follow the mutual fund world in depth, this forty-eight-page monthly newsletter is a relatively inexpensive way to do it. What I like about this publication is that it not only keeps you up-to-date with news about funds and the financial markets, it also runs feature stories on specific funds and fund families, a "What's That?" section that explains investing terms and strategies, and a regular "Planners Corner" department that shows how real people are grappling with real investing issues. The newsletter also provides reams of performance stats on all of Morningstar's fund categories and on five hundred specific funds.

No-Load Fund Investor ($129 a year for new subcribers; $65 for a six-month subscription; 800-252-2042): This twenty-page monthly letter covers only no-load funds (that is, ones that don't charge sales commissions), which isn't a problem as far as I'm concerned. Editor Sheldon Jacobs does a commendable job of keeping his subscribers up-to-date with news and commentary on the financial markets and fund world, provides performance stats on about eight hundred funds, and offers three model portfolios—one for capital growth, another for income, and the third a combination of capital growth and income—that can serve as guidelines for building your own mix of funds.

FOR STOCK INVESTORS

Morningstar Stock Investor ($79 a year for twelve issues; 800-735-0700): Okay, call me a shill for Morningstar since I'm mentioning another of the company's newsletters, and a new one at that. (*Stock Investor* was launched in May 1998.) But the reason I like this thirty-page newsletter is that, much like the company's fund newsletter described earlier, it's written with the individual investor in mind. It offers news and commentary on the financial markets, short articles on specific stocks, a "Workshop" section that makes sense of investing terms like *free cash flow* (no, it's not a rallying cry to get cash flow out of the slammer), and stories describing the investment strategies of well-known investors.

FOR FUND AND/OR STOCK INVESTORS

Richard C. Young's Intelligence Report ($99.95 for twelve issues; 800-301-8969): I've been a reader of Dick Young's various newsletters for more than a decade, and I've always found his newsletter an enjoyable read, during which you also pick up good sound investing advice. A veteran of more than thirty years on the investing scene, Young is not one to get swept up in market fads and hype. Instead he homes in on undervalued sectors and other areas of the market that the Wall Street herd overlooks. (You won't find many other newsletters writing about values in mundane water company stocks, as Young has.) I also like his approach to funds: invest in an S&P 500 index fund as the core of your portfolio and go with no-load, low-expense funds from there. One more thing: Young is also a fan of early rock and roll, so don't be surprised if you find insights on Duane "Rebel Rouser" Eddie mixed among those on stocks and funds.

INVESTMENT SERVICES FOR HARD-CORE INVESTORS: MORNINGSTAR AND VALUE LINE

If you really want to get down to the nitty-gritty details about a fund's investing style and its historical performance, you should take a look at Morningstar Mutual Funds, a subscription service that provides reports and analyses on more than 1,600 funds. The detailed one-page reports Morningstar provides are updated quarterly, while recent performance statistics on all the funds as well as a commentary on funds and the market are mailed out every two weeks. If you're not used to delving into this kind of information, it can be pretty daunting and, if you're not a numbers junkie, a bit dull. Each report is brimming with statistics on the fund's returns and risk, a short analysis of the fund by a Morningstar fund analyst, a look at the fund's most recent holdings, a look at portfolio statistics—in short, the kind of stuff that would appeal to a fund fanatic but turn off most ordinary people. This service isn't cheap: a yearly subscription goes for $425, although a less comprehensive version covering about seven hundred or so no-load funds is available for $175. You might be able to get by without springing for a subscription, though, since many public libraries carry this service.

VALUE LINE INVESTMENT SURVEY: MORE THAN YOU WANTED TO KNOW ABOUT 1,700 STOCKS

You should have no trouble these days getting enough stock statistics to thoroughly confuse yourself; it's one of the joys of the information age. But one service that pulls together an impressive array of stock data and actually puts it into a manageable form useful even for beginning investors is the Value Line Investment Survey. Basically the survey has three parts. First, there's the "Summary & Index" section, which provides market information and industry stats as well as updated performance data on the stocks covered by the survey. This section includes a variety of screens that highlight stocks that might be of interest to certain types of investors. For growth investors, for example, there's a "high growth" screen that lists stocks that have had average growth rates of 13 percent or more over the past ten years and that Value Line expects to grow at a 13 percent or better pace over the next five years. There's also a screen of possibly undervalued stocks—that is, ones whose recent prices are low in relation to their book value or the value of their underlying net worth. Following this section, there's the "Selection & Opinion" section, which offers analysis about the markets and economy from Value Line's analysts, as well as reports on a few companies that the analysts consider particularly attractive at the moment. Both of these sections are updated every week, and presumably there are people who subscribe to the service for these sections alone because of the investing leads they provide.

But to my mind the best reason to consult Value Line is for the one-page information-packed reports the survey provides on the 1,700 companies it covers. (For investors who want to trawl for very small stocks, there's an expanded version that covers an extra 1,800 issues.) These reports are updated just four times a year, so you'll want to check out the "Summary & Index" section as well as other sources for the most recent stock prices, price-earnings ratios, and other statistics. But the reason they're worth consulting even if they don't have up-to-the-minute data is that they pull together into one place a detailed look at each company's financial and operating history dating back as long as fifteen years. That convenience doesn't come cheap—the survey costs $570 a year—although you can find Value Line in many large public libraries as well as in some brokerage offices. Of course, you could also gather much of this historical data yourself from other sources—annual reports, various Web sites, and so forth. But doing so for just one stock could take several days, and compiling such a financial profile on even a handful of stocks could take several weeks. Presumably you've got better things to do with your time.

INVESTING WITH YOUR COMPUTER: SIZING UP SOFTWARE

There's no doubt your computer can help you acquire and massage massive amounts of data on stocks and funds. Whether it can also help you earn better returns is another question. But if you're convinced your PC can give you an edge—or you just get a kick out of slicing and dicing investment data on your PC— here are a few of the top fund- and stock-investing CD programs, along with brief descriptions of what each can do:

Principia for Mutual Funds ($395 a year for monthly updates; $195 for quarterly updates; 800-735-0700): This Morningstar program gives you scads of information about more than 8,500 funds that you can sort by 130 different criteria, ranging from past performance over a variety of periods to risk to annual expenses.

American Association of Individual Investors Quarterly Low-Load Mutual Fund Update ($39 a year for AAII members, $50 for non-members for information on about 800 funds; 800-428-2244): This software program doesn't cover as many funds, provide as much detail on those it does cover, or have the same screening capacity as Morningstar's *Principia* . . . but it's a lot cheaper and, unlike all the other software programs mentioned in this chapter, it works on a Mac. Not a bad program to start with.

Value Line Investment Survey for Windows ($595 a year for 1,700 stocks; CDs are updated monthly, weekly online; $995 for 5,000 stocks; 800-535-8760): The print version of Value Line offers you ready-made screens, including lists of stocks with low price-earnings ratios or low price-to-book ratios. With the CD-ROM program, however, you're seated at the mighty Wurlitzer, so you get to play the tunes, mixing and matching screens until you come up with a list of stocks that meet a variety of criteria.

Morningstar StockTools ($375 a year for quarterly updates, $675 for monthly updates on more than eight thousand stocks; 800-735-0700): As with *Principia for Mutual Funds,* you can splice, dice, rank, and graph stocks by a variety of statistics, including ever-popular indicators such as price-earnings ratios, market caps, total returns, earnings estimates, price momentum—pretty much anything a stock stat junkie would want to do. With *StockTools* you also get a subscription to the monthly stock newsletter *Morningstar Stock Investor.*

American Association of Individual Investors Stock Investor ($99 a year for members, $147 for nonmembers for quarterly updates on about 8,800 companies; *Pro* version has expanded data and monthly updates, $198 a year for members, $247 for nonmembers; 800-428-2244): This little program offers scads of stock data at a bargain price. You get everything from earnings estimates to income statements and balance sheets to price-earnings ratios and cash-flow statements to insider buy and sell decisions—up to 1,500 data fields per company. And since you can screen on the basis of all this information, you can spend hours, days, months, in front of your computer screen, looking for that magical combination of statistics that can lead you to winning stocks. (If you find such a combination, let me know.) Unlike the American

Association of Individual Investors' mutual fund CD-ROM, though, this one's for PCs only.

GREATEST HITS ON THE WEB

In its zeal to look hip, the financial press often overstates the role the Web should play in your investment strategy, suggesting you should hang out in chat rooms to glean insights about a company's prospects or to get advance warning of problems that may push down a company's stock price. The implication is that by trolling the Web for the latest news or investing info and acting on it, you can get an edge on the market.

It doesn't take a genius to see this is pure nonsense. For one thing, there are virtually no standards for posting information and advice on the Web. Web sites from established investment firms exist a click away from sites set up by blowhards, know-nothings, short sellers spreading false rumors about a company's imminent demise, and outright hustlers, and sometimes it's hard to tell one from another (especially since the sites of major financial firms can also contain high levels of bombast). Even if the information you're getting is reliable, it's not as if you're getting it before anyone else. Somebody had to post it on the Web in the first place. And suppose you do get a jump on the crowd; are you sure you know how the market will react to the news? Even if you get *that* one right, will the movement be enough to compensate you for the transaction costs of trading?

That said, there are some worthwhile sites that can provide news and good basic data, ranging from stats on funds' returns and risks to detailed financial information that can help you evaluate the performance and prospects of individual companies. In short, information that is consistent with choosing and monitoring investments that you plan to hold on to for the long term, not flip every few days. If you're looking for that kind of information, consider the following ten sites. All are free, except Standard & Poor's Personal Wealth, which charges $9.95 a month.

TEN WEB SITES WORTH A VISIT

Yahoo Finance (www.yahoofinance.com): This site offers an impressive array of basic info and services, including portfolio tracking, recent news stories, and financial data on companies; a glossary of investing terms; and links to thousands of other financial sites. This is a good place to start your search for information on stocks and funds.

Invest-O-Rama (www.investorama.com): Run by *Investor's Web Guide* author Douglas Gerlach, this site of sites features links to almost 8,000 investing sites in 80 categories, ranging from stock screening to a directory of 4,500 public companies to articles and advice on how to get started investing.

Standard & Poor's Personal Wealth (www.personalwealth. com): You pay $9.95 a month for access to this site, but for that price you get to tap into an awful lot: daily market news, access to data and analysis on some 9,500 companies and 8,500 mutual funds, and a customized home page that lets you track the prices of and get updates on your investments. The most ballyhooed feature of the page is the one I think you've also got to use most carefully and sparingly—personalized buy, hold, and sell recommendations for stocks and mutual funds based on your investment goals and current holdings.

Quicken (www.quicken.com/investment): Managed by the maker of the popular Quicken personal finance software, this site offers a broad but not very deep array of investment info, such as basic searches for stocks and funds, market commentary, and corporate earnings estimates. At other sections of the site, you can shop for insurance and mortgages, do basic retirement planning, and, if you wish, file your taxes.

Morningstar.net (www.morningstar.net): Hands down, the best site on the Web to get raw data on funds and keep up with news about the fund world, although as of mid-1998 the site's fund screening tool was woefully weak. You'll also want to check out Morningstar's X-ray feature. You enter all your fund holdings, and voilà! You get such information as the average expense ratio, sector weightings, and mix of stocks, bonds, and cash for your entire portfolio. Morningstar offers commentary and educational pieces at the site as well and seems to be bulking up its stock coverage.

Mutual Fund Investor's Center (www.mfea.com): A great site to learn about both the basics and the finer points of investing in funds, including the ins and outs of fund taxation and risk tolerance. The site was created by a trade group of no-load fund companies known as the Mutual Fund Education Alliance, so, as you might expect, it pushes the gospel of no-load investing. As a convert to that school of investing, I see no big harm in a little proselytizing along those lines.

Fund Alarm (www.fundalarm.com): This site is probably best known for its list of three-alarm funds—that is, ones that have underperformed their appropriate benchmarks over the past one, three, and five years. But I check in occasionally mostly because I enjoy the way site creator Roy Weitz wittily skewers fund managers and fund execs for various blunders, inane statements, and self-serving moves.

Market Player (www.marketplayer.com): One of the best stock screens on the Web. Want to identify stocks that have increased earnings at least 15 percent annually the past five years but have PE ratios below the market average? You can develop such a list—for whatever it's worth—here. Of course, you'll have to learn how to use a quirky screening system that's based on a code even a master spy might have trouble deciphering—but, hey, what do you expect when you get something free?

Daily Stocks (www.dailystocks.com): Great starting point for research on a company and its stock. Enter the company name or ticker symbol—say, General Electric—and a page pops up with hypertext links to everything from a one-page report on the company chock full of stock and financial performance data, news stories on GE from sources as diverse as CNET/Bloomberg to *Time* magazine, GE investor forums and chat rooms— even quotes on GE options. Sure, many of the links are a waste of your time, but there's plenty of solid information there, too.

American Association of Individual Investors (www.aaii. org): A good place to learn the basics about investing and building a portfolio of stocks, bonds, and funds—and to read about the more sophisticated strategies of such well-known investors as Peter Lynch, David Dreman, and the late value guru Benjamin Graham. I found the site kind of clunky and irritating to navigate, but the material AAII offers here really can improve your investing skills. Best of all, the info is presented in a simple, straightforward way, a refreshing change from the manic graphics and hype that dominate other sites.

CHAPTER 10

An Irreverent–But Accurate–Glossary of Investing Terms

• • • • • • • • • • •

Given the tendency of stockbrokers, money managers, financial planners, and other investment pros to speak in their own unintelligible patois, you will from time to time come across unfamiliar and sometimes downright puzzling terms. Not to worry. Just consider it part of Wall Street's quirky charm that stringing together sentences laden with technical jargon and other mumbo-jumbo is what often passes for investing intellect.

In this section you will find realistic definitions for investment terms that you are likely to come across on your own or that may be inflicted upon you by an investment jockey trying to impress you with his knowledge of things financial. I say the definitions I offer are "realistic" because in some cases the definitions you find in investment reference books amount to a sort of bogus construct—that is to say, the definition reflects little more than what investment professionals have decided the word will mean, which often leaves out more critical interpretations. In short, in the following list I try to tell you what many of these terms mean, and what they really mean.

account executive: one of many aliases that brokers go by rather than simply calling themselves brokers. Other euphemistic tags preferred by brokers include financial consultant, financial adviser, and the unbelievably pretentious personal CFO (chief financial officer).

aggressive growth fund: a fund that takes above-average risks in search of above-average returns. You'll get the above-average risks no matter which aggressive fund you choose, but only the good funds also give you the oversize returns. Aggressive growth funds typically invest in shares of companies whose revenues and profits are growing at a rapid rate; they may also trade shares frequently, invest in stock market indexes and options, and employ risky strategies like borrowing money to buy securities (this is known as leveraging) or selling short, a technique that allows investors to profit on falling stock prices by borrowing securities, selling them, and then (if things work out) replacing them at a cheaper price.

annual report: reports that companies and mutual funds send to shareholders to bring them up-to-date on the firm's or fund's recent performance. Typically, in this report the company chief executive officer or fund manager takes credit for terrific performance—or explains how he made the best of a bad situation if the company or fund has lagged. You'll find lots of financial data in annual reports but rarely much critical self-evaluation or candor.

asset allocation: a fancy word that means don't put all your eggs in one basket; the process of dividing up your holdings among stocks (or stock funds), bonds (or bond funds), and money-market funds and then largely holding that mix constant regardless of market conditions. Not to be confused with the term *tactical asset allocation,* which (naively, in my opinion) advocates changing your mix to capitalize on market conditions.

asset allocation fund: a fund that practices asset allocation (see previous entry) by diversifying holdings, typically among stocks, bonds, and cash equivalents such as Treasury bills and short-term corporate IOUs called *commercial paper.*

averaging down: a "strategy" brokers advocate when the price of a stock they've recommended takes a dive. The idea is if you bought, say, one hundred shares at $10 and the stock has dropped to $5, buying another hundred shares will bring your average cost to $7.50 a share. Of course, all the averaging down in the world means nothing if the stock doesn't eventually recover.

back-end load: a way to make a fund with a sales commission look as though it doesn't have one; this illusion is pulled off by levying a sales charge if you withdraw money from the fund within a certain number of years instead of when you put it in. Also known as *contingent deferred sales charges,* back-end loads usually start at 5 percent or 6 percent if you pull out your money within a year of investing in the fund and then decline by a percentage point or so each year until they disappear.

balanced fund: no, not the opposite of a lopsided fund; rather, a fund that keeps 50 percent to 60 percent of its assets in stocks (usually dividend-paying shares) and 40 percent to 50 percent in bonds, although the manager generally has the authority to change those proportions if he wishes. These funds typically have the highest yields of all stock funds because of the interest payments and dividends generated by the portfolio's bonds and stocks.

bear market: a 20 percent or better decline in stock prices, as measured by a market benchmark like the Dow Jones Industrial Average or Standard & Poor's 500 index. The most amazing thing about bear markets isn't that they occur, but the lengths that some investment advisers and personal finance publications will go to to claim they predicted the bear's arrival in advance.

beta: a handy word to throw around when you want to appear as though you're really a savvy investor; a statistical barometer of risk used mostly for stocks and funds that measures how much a stock's or fund's value fluctuates relative to a standard benchmark—typically the Standard & Poor's 500 stock index. By definition, the S&P 500's beta equals 1, so a fund with a beta of 1.1 would be expected to gain 10 percent more than the S&P 500 when stock prices are rising and fall 10 percent more when stock prices drop.

broker: the name to call a broker when you want to get his dander up.

callable bond: *not* a bond for which you have the option of calling the company to make sure they plan on repaying it on time; a callable bond is one the issuer can repay before the end of its term. Issuers usually exercise the right to repay early if interest rates have dropped since the bond was issued. The call date tells you when the issuer can begin to exercise that right.

capital gain (or loss): profit (or loss) that occurs when the price of an investment climbs above (or drops below) its purchase price. You have a realized capital gain or loss if you actually sell the security for a price above or below what you paid.

capital gains distribution: a payment a mutual fund makes to shareholders from the profits a fund realizes when it sells securities for more than it paid for them. Capital gains are generally paid out once at the end of the year. One of the screwier things about the way mutual funds operate is that a fund can have a loss for a year yet still pay out capital gains for that year. Result: Even though your fund lost money, it's possible that you could have to shell out taxes on the gains the fund posted when it sold securities at a profit.

cash equivalents: Wall Street jargon for short-term debt securities such as Treasury bills, commercial paper, and money-market funds. Such investments are referred to as *cash equivalents* (or even simply *cash*) because they can be converted quickly to cash.

contingent deferred sales charge: see *back-end load*.

convertible bond: hermaphrodite of the securities world, a bond that contains characteristics of both stocks and bonds. A convertible bond can be cashed in for shares of stock in the company that issued the bond.

corporate bond fund: a fund that invests in bonds and other debt securities issued by corporations—in other words, a bond fund that invests in corporate IOUs.

correction: the euphemism market professionals use to describe a setback of 10 percent to 20 percent in stock, typically as measured by an index like the Dow Jones Industrial Average or Standard & Poor's 500. (Once prices fall 20 percent or more, the correction becomes a "bear market.") As with many Wall Street terms, this one has a twisted logic to it. If the market has "corrected" by falling 10 percent, that must mean the market was somehow "wrong" when stock prices were higher—and you were 10 percent richer.

credit risk: the risk you'll get stiffed on interest or principal payments by the company or government agency that issued the bond. To evaluate that risk, check the bond's rating from ratings companies like Standard & Poor's or Moody's Investors Service.

dead-cat bounce: Term money managers use to describe a weak, ineffective rebound following a big market crash. Term originates from the macabre notion that if you drop it from high enough, a dead cat will bounce, even though there's no life in it.

derivative: an investment whose value is derived from some other asset, index, interest rate, or benchmark; some derivatives are highly risky, others are more benign and are used mainly as hedging devices to lower risk. Funny, fund managers and other money managers rarely admit to using the toxic variety of derivatives.

distribution yield: a way for bond funds to give you the impression you're getting a higher yield than you actually are; this smoke-and-mirrors effect is pulled off by returning your own capital to you but making it seem as though you're getting an interest or dividend payment.

dividend: the payment some companies make to holders of their stock or that a fund makes to shareholders from interest payments the fund receives from bonds or dividends paid by the stocks in the fund's portfolios. The upside to dividends is that you've gotten some money out of your investment. The downside: Uncle Sam wants a cut of that dividend in the form of taxes.

dollar-cost averaging: the technique of investing the same dollar amount at regular intervals—say, monthly. Contrary to popular perceptions, dollar-cost averaging doesn't assure you'll get the highest returns, nor does it prevent you from getting hammered during market declines. The discipline of regular investing can, however, help prevent you from dumping most of your money into the market when share prices and investor euphoria are unrealistically high and thus vulnerable to a setback.

"Don't fight the tape": A phrase brokers use to sell stocks to clients who are worried that soaring stock prices might be pushing the market into dangerously overvalued territory. The phrase is a holdover from the days when brokers actually followed stock prices on ticker tape. Another version of this "If you can't beat 'em, join 'em" sentiment: "The trend is your friend."

duration: a technical measure of a bond or bond fund's sensitivity to interest rate fluctuations that takes into account bonds' average maturity, the possibility of early redemptions, and interest payments. The actual formula is too complicated and boring to go into, but the higher the duration, the more volatile the bond.

earnings yield: Earnings per share divided by the current stock price; the opposite of the price-earnings ratio. A stock with annual earnings of $2 and a price of $40 would have an earnings yield of 5 percent and a PE of 20. In general, the lower the earnings yield, the riskier the stock, because investors are putting a lot of faith on future earnings to provide a return.

equity-income fund: an incredibly imprecise term to describe a fund that invests in a mix of bonds and dividend-paying stocks. Growth-and-income funds also invest in a blend of stocks and bonds, which only goes to show that the naming of some mutual fund categories is more art than science.

expense ratio: a way to tell how deep the fund company's hand is going into your pocket; the expense ratio is the fund's total annual expenses expressed as a percentage of average net assets.

Fannie Mae: One of the belles of the mortgage-backed bond world. For details, see *Ginnie Mae.*

financial planner: two of the most dangerous words in the personal finance industry, largely because this term can be used by financial advisers who are knowledgeable about investments and have high ethical standards and by incompetents, clowns, and crooks looking to separate you from your money.

front-end load: the sales charge levied by some funds at the time of purchase—that is, a transfer of money from you to a broker or financial planner selling the fund. Brokers would have you believe that the load, or sales commission, compensates them for the research that led them to recommend the fund; cynics would say the prospect of a commission had more to do with the recommendation than research.

Ginnie Mae: the name may conjure up an image of a *Gone With the Wind* Southern belle in a frilly hoop dress, but a Ginnie Mae is actually just slang for a security issued by the Government National Mortgage Association, or GNMA (hence, Ginnie Mae). Ginnie Maes are essentially shares in a pool of mortgages guaranteed by the GNMA, which is a government-sponsored corporation. Similar securities, Fannie Maes, are issued by the Federal National Mortgage Association (FNMA).

government bond fund: a fund that invests in U.S. government securities, ranging from Treasury notes and bonds to Ginnie Maes and Fannie Maes. Under current law, funds can call themselves government bond funds even if they hold up to 35 percent of their assets in nongovernment bonds. The Securities and Exchange Commission has proposed revising that standard to 20 percent. An improvement, yes, but not nearly as tough as the standard required to use the phrase "all-beef hot dogs."

growth fund: a fund that aims for capital appreciation, typically by buying shares of fast-growing companies or shares of companies whose assets are undervalued. Since most growth funds fail to outperform market benchmarks like the Standard & Poor's 500 index over extended periods, "stunted growth fund" would be a more apt term for most of them.

high-yield fund: the "accentuate the positive" euphemism that clever fund industry marketing executives have developed for junk bond funds; name for a bond fund that invests in bonds that are below investment grade (aka junk bonds).

index fund: a fund designed to track the performance of a market benchmark like the Standard & Poor's 500 stock index. When fund managers beat index funds, they brag about their investing prowess; when managers trail index funds, they claim it's inappropriate to compare their fund to the index.

initial public offering (IPO): the first time a company's stock is offered to the public; brokers peddling these offerings may try to convince you that IPO means "instant profit opportunity," but it more likely stands for "it's probably overpriced." In my opinion, much of the IPO market is rigged one way or another and should be avoided unless you're an insider.

interest rate risk: the chance rising interest rates will pummel the value of a bond or a bond fund.

intermediate-term bond (or bond fund): a bond scheduled to repay its principal within four to ten years or a fund that buys bonds with maturities in that range. If you're looking for decent income without a whole lot of shaking going on in the price of the bond or bond fund, you're probably better off sticking with intermediate-term bonds.

international fund: a fund that invests in securities issued outside the United States—aka a foreign fund. A *global* fund, on the other hand, invests in foreign securities but also has the option to buy American.

junk bond fund: see *high-yield fund*.

long-term bond (or bond fund): a bond scheduled to be repaid ten or more years in the future; a bond fund that invests primarily in such bonds. Long-term bonds typically have the highest yields and offer a shot at the highest gains. But they get mangled the most when interest rates fall.

management fee: the (sometimes exorbitant) fee paid to a money manager or a fund's investment adviser for choosing and monitoring the securities in the portfolio; mutual fund directors, who are supposed to be advocates for fund shareholders, have an unnerving habit of approving management fee hikes every time the investment adviser requests them, even though common sense would suggest higher fees are not in the fund shareholders' interests.

market timing: a form of investing hocus-pocus that involves moving all or most of one's money back and forth between stocks or stock funds and cash or money-market funds in a vain attempt to ride the stock market up and jump out before it tanks; the only thing this ingenious strategy is missing is evidence that it actually works.

maturity: a concept applied to bonds (though definitely *not* bond traders); in investing parlance, maturity is the number of years before a bond's principal, or face amount, must be repaid. The longer the maturity, the more the price of a bond will increase (or decrease) when interest rates drop (or rise).

money-market fund: a type of mutual fund that invests in very short-term debt securities, such as Treasury bills and corporate IOUs (aka commercial paper). Overall, money funds are generally as safe a stash for your cash as a bank account (if that's any comfort).

multiple: slang for PE ratio that investors and journalists use when they want you to think they really know what they're talking about, as in, "Hey, that market multiple's really getting scary."

municipal bond (or bond fund): Muni bonds, tax-exempt securities issued by states, cities, and other local governments, as well as a variety of government agencies, everything from housing authorities (housing bonds) to municipal water systems (water and sewer bonds). A muni bond fund is a mutual fund that invests in these securities.

mutual fund: the investment craze of the nineties; technically a mutual fund is a company that pools money from investors and buys securities such as stocks, bonds, or money-market instruments.

National Association of Securities Dealers: a brokerage industry organization that regulates and sometimes disciplines brokers; the NASD also oversees the marketing and advertising of mutual funds; depending on your view, the NASD's existence is an indication that the brokerage industry is capable of disciplining itself and keeping the industry clean or proof that self-regulatory organizations are too self-serving to provide any meaningful regulation of themselves.

net asset value: aka the NAV, this is the value of a share of a mutual fund. It's calculated by taking all the fund's assets, subtracting any liabilities (such as money the fund owes if it has borrowed any), and then dividing the result by the number of fund shares issued. This is the price you pay when you buy shares (unless the fund charges a load, in which case you buy at the "offering price," which includes the load) and the price you get when you sell shares (unless the fund deducts a redemption fee or deferred sales charge).

no-load: a fund that charges no up-front or back-end sales commission—in other words, the kind you should try to buy whenever possible if you are picking your own funds.

North American Securities Administrators Association: NASAA (pronounced Naa-suh, like the space agency) is an organization of state securities regulators that can help you check a broker's or financial planner's background to see if he or she has been disciplined for ethical or legal actions or has any such complaints pending.

option: the right, but not the obligation, to buy or sell a security in the future. Options have legitimate uses—farmers can use corn or wheat options to hedge against the possibility of falling crop prices—but they're also pushed as what amounts to a form of legal gambling to speculate on the future path of stock or commodity prices.

portfolio: the term many people mistakenly apply to the haphazard collection of stocks, bonds, and/or mutual funds they own; a true portfolio is a group of securities chosen to work in concert with each other to achieve a specific financial goal.

portfolio turnover: a barometer of how frequently a fund manager buys and sells securities. A fund with an annual turnover rate of 100 percent effectively replaces its entire portfolio in one year. Most U.S. stock funds have turnover rates of about 75 percent. Quick-draw managers often—but not always—generate lots of taxable capital gains that raise your tax bill and lower your effective return.

price-earnings ratio: stock price divided by earnings, so a measure of what investors are willing to pay for earnings. The higher the PE ratio, generally the hotter the stock—and the harder it will fall if future earnings disappoint investors or the market overall heads south. A major growth industry on Wall Street is coming up with rationalizations suggesting that bloated PE ratios really aren't an indication that the stock market is overheated and overvalued.

prospectus: exceedingly boring document or booklet written by and seemingly for lawyers that provides financial details and information on the operation of a company or, in the case of a mutual fund, info such as the fund's investing strategy, fees, and policies on matters such as additional investments and redemptions.

redemption fee: a fee that may actually be good for investors; typically 0.25 percent to 1 percent, a redemption fee is imposed on withdrawals from a fund to discourage hyper investors from jumping in and out of a fund, creating transaction costs that erode returns. Unlike a back-end sales charge, redemption fees usually go back into the fund, not to a salesperson.

Russell 2000 index: a widely followed index consisting of the stocks of two thousand small U.S. companies; a benchmark to gauge the performance of small stocks and small-stock funds.

sector fund: the mutual fund version of gambling; you figure out which sector of the market is going to be hot—although how you do this, I don't know—and then buy a fund that specializes in that industry. Fidelity Investments has the dubious distinction of being the sultan of the sector market, with about thirty-five different sector portfolios, many seemingly plying the same waters (Fidelity Select-Energy, Fidelity Select-Energy Services, Fidelity Select-Natural Gas).

Securities and Exchange Commission: the federal agency that enforces securities laws such as the Securities Act of 1933, the Investment Company Act of 1940 (which governs mutual funds), and a bunch of other acts that are supposed to give individual investors a fighting chance at not getting screwed in the securities market. The SEC does a credible job overall, but a highly developed sense of skepticism is still your best first line of defense.

short-term bond (or bond fund): a bond with an average maturity of two to four years, or a bond fund investing in such bonds; a place to put your money if you want to minimize damage from rising interest rates.

small-company fund: in theory, a fund that primarily buys shares of small companies, typically those with stock market values of $1 billion or less. In reality, many funds that start out buying small companies attract so much money that they can no longer buy small companies. The manager then spends most of his or her time explaining that the fund is really still a small-stock fund even though it owns medium-size stocks.

Standard & Poor's 500 stock index: an index of five hundred stocks of large U.S. companies in a variety of industries that is put together by a bunch of people at investment research firm Standard & Poor's. Although it sounds like a competitor to the Indy 500, the S&P 500 is actually a decent benchmark for gauging overall activity in the U.S. stock market.

standard deviation: a measure of risk that tells you how much a fund's returns bounce around. The higher a fund's standard deviation, the more volatile—and riskier—the fund is. Ask three investment experts how standard deviation is calculated, and I bet you get at least six answers.

systematic withdrawal plan: this term could refer to the way brokers and other advisers separate clients from their money, but it's really a program offered by many funds in which shareholders receive payments from their accounts (either fixed dollar amounts or a percentage of assets) on a regular basis, usually monthly.

technical analysis: a form of financial voodoo in which "analysts" chart any number of statistics, such as individual stock prices, market indexes, and trading volume, in an attempt to divine future movements in a stock or the market overall. If you believe in astrology, you'll love technical analysis.

total return: the most comprehensive measure of performance of a stock or fund. In the case of a stock, total return includes any increase or decrease in the stock's price and assumes that dividends, if any, were reinvested in additional shares of the stock. In the case of funds, total return reflects increases or decreases in the price of the fund shares and assumes that any capital gains, interest, and dividends that were distributed were invested in additional shares of the fund when paid. Total return is generally the best gauge for comparing the performance of two investments.

Treasury securities: debt issued by the U.S. Treasury. These securities can be Treasury bills (maturity of one year or less), notes (maturity of two to ten years), and bonds (maturities of ten to thirty years). These are considered the safest investments on the planet—at least in terms of guaranteeing repayment of your original principal—since they are backed by the full faith and credit of the U.S. government.

12b–1 fee: an annual expense, usually 0.25 percent to 1 percent of the fund's assets, that funds charge shareholders to pay for the costs of selling the fund—that is, reimbursing the fund company for marketing and sales expenses. This fee is also sometimes appropriately called the *hidden load* because many investors don't realize they're paying it.

yield: the basic measure of the income a stock, bond, or fund pays investors. Yield is one of those stats that can be manipulated pretty easily. For a bond, the best measure is yield to maturity—in other words, what the bond would pay on an annual basis if you buy it now and hold it till it matures. For a bond fund, check out its *SEC yield,* also known as its *thirty-day yield,* a figure that tells you how much income the fund has paid over the past thirty days as a percentage of the fund's net asset value. As for stocks, the yield is simply the total of the dividends paid over the most recent four quarters divided by the current stock price.

zero–coupon bond: a bond that pays no current interest; zeros are sold at a large discount to their face value and are repaid at face value when they mature. Zeros appeal to two distinctly different types of investors. Since you know exactly how much you'll get back when the bond matures (assuming it doesn't default), investors who want the certainty of having a specific amount of money at a specific time often buy zeros. But since the price of zeros (and especially long-term zeros) fluctuates much more than the price of conventional interest-paying bonds, zeros also appeal to gamblers and speculators who (foolishly, in my opinion) believe they can predict the direction of interest rates and grab big capital gains in the process.

INDEX

INDEX

INDEX

249

INDEX

INDEX

INDEX

INDEX

INDEX

ABOUT THE AUTHOR

WALTER UPDEGRAVE is a financial expert and a senior editor at *Money* magazine. Over the past fifteen years, he has won numerous journalism awards for his work at *Money* as well as other publications, and has appeared as a guest on *The Oprah Winfrey Show, Today, CBS This Morning*, CNN, CNBC, and numerous local TV and radio shows. He is also the author of *The Right Way to Invest in Mutual Funds* and *How to Keep Your Savings Safe*. Updegrave received an economics degree from the University of Pennsylvania, but has never let that obstacle prevent him from bringing wit, humor, and commonsense analysis to personal finance. A Philadelphia native and longtime "Iggles" fan, he now lives with his wife and son in New Rochelle, New York, the very same hometown of Rob and Laura Petrie of *The Dick Van Dyke Show*.